LOCAL HISTORY
ON THE GROUND

LOCAL HISTORY
ON THE GROUND

TOM WELSH

First published 2009

The History Press
The Mill, Brimscombe Port
Stroud, Gloucestershire, GL5 2QG
www.thehistorypress.co.uk

© Tom Welsh, 2009

The right of Tom Welsh to be identified as the Author
of this work has been asserted in accordance with the
Copyrights, Designs and Patents Act 1988.

British Library Cataloguing in Publication Data.
A catalogue record for this book is available from the British Library.

ISBN 978 0 7524 4798 8

Typesetting and origination by The History Press
Printed in Great Britain

CONTENTS

ACKNOWLEDGEMENTS

I would like to acknowledge the support of Dr Robin Crockett at the University of Northampton for his services in enhancing colour plates 1, 2, 10, 15 and 21, which would otherwise have been unusable, and my brother Charles Welsh for plate 20. I would also like to acknowledge *Yorkshire Archaeology Journal*, Archaeology North-West and Hampshire Field Club Newsletter for permission to re-use Figures 25, 46, 47 and 10. Figure 1 and colour plate 6 bear acknowledgements for permission to use or redraw Ordnance Survey maps. The book draws on forty years of fieldwork, during which time the author received invaluable help from many local historians and amateur archaeologists who shared their skills and knowledge. This is also an opportunity to thank all the landowners and tenant farmers for their goodwill in letting me explore their land.

Chapter One

DISPELLING THE MYTHS

It may be that I share W.G. Hoskin's good fortune in having grown up in an interesting locality, at the intersection of several parishes, that offered so much inspiration. Hoskins, in his introduction to fieldwork, subtitled 'A Backwoods Parish', described Cadbury in Devon, where he spent frequent holidays with relatives, and the readily accessible countryside around his several home towns.[1] This was the basis for his explorations. My own home parishes were on the south of Glasgow, similarly accessible countryside within a short walk from where I lived, which triggered a deep-seated interest in the history of my familiar landscape. The difference – apart from the intervening half a century – was that I became more interested in the evidence of the past on the ground, in the form of bumps and hollows, supported by documentary research, whereas most would-be local historians follow a mostly documentary route.

Half a century did make a difference though, in that Hoskins' backwoods parish had seen little change for decades. My own, at first on the fringes of expanding Glasgow, was rapidly being filled by new estates and new infrastructure, with the urbanised fringe migrating steadily southwards, so my explorations had to keep ahead of change. Perhaps that gave added stimulus to explore. Right from the very beginning I was finding evidence or visiting known earthworks that were being damaged or destroyed within months or years. Eventually I was able to write a history of these four parishes,[2] and significantly for this book, it was one that combined the history on the ground with the history in the documents. That was nearly twenty years ago, but this writer has continued to advocate integrated historical research and fieldwork. The intention of the present book is to help the local historian combine history with an understanding of physical remains in modern landscapes. That is why this book is entitled *Local History on the Ground*.

What is 'local history on the ground'?

A useful analogy to local history on the ground can be made with family history research. Television has transformed genealogy by adding the 'on the ground' dimension, with such programmes as *Who do you think you are?* These programmes add an extra dimension to tracing your ancestors by guiding their celebrity subjects to the places where their ancestors lived; looking for the actual buildings if they survive; seeing the landscapes in which they lived, and latter-day evidence of the trades in which they engaged. The viewer shares the experience of seeing key documents and old photographs in the places where the research was carried out. The writer, in his own family history searches, has done much the same, visiting the places where ancestors lived, and trying to get a feel for their world. There is one limitation to this. The landscape seen is the modern landscape, and we are asked to imagine what it was like a hundred or two hundred years ago. We might get to see an extant house that has been much changed over time, or the ruins or grassed-over remains where the house stood. We see a landscape, but the way it is farmed or managed may be significantly different from the way it appeared to the people who lived there centuries ago. With local history we engage in much the same kind of speculation and imagination. The community or landscape explored is seen as it is today, and we have to try to see it as it was. This book is about finding and interpreting the clues to that past landscape.

It is also important, right from the start, to make a distinction between this local history on the ground and the landscape history or archaeology popularised in recent decades. Sometime in the 1970s or 1980s, landscape archaeology, which was supposed to go hand in hand with local history, parted company and became something on its own. This book therefore adopts a stance different from conventional landscape history and archaeology, in order to restore some of the benefits of fieldwork to local historians. It is about reading history from the surviving physical evidence, not necessarily recording archaeology. The book is directed, unashamedly, at the humble and often apparently inexplicable pattern of hummocks and hollows still to be found somewhere, in almost every parish, that haven't yet been explained. It is aimed at readers who, at one time or other, have stopped and looked and puzzled over features seen, which have captured their curiosity but are not readily explicable. And the intention of the book is to help the reader make sense of them, while drawing upon other local history resources at the same time.

So how did local history and local archaeology part company? They were quite synonymous in the 1960s when Hoskins and another early pioneer, Maurice Beresford, were putting forward their ideas. *Beresford's History on the Ground*, first published in 1957,[3] and its predecessor *The Lost Villages in England* in 1954,[4] directly tackled the remains of deserted villages, or old estate boundaries and landscaped parks, and inspired a succession of books by other writers on similar themes. Both Hoskins and Beresford looked at landscapes through the eyes of historians, drawing on a variety of documentary resources to elucidate the landscape. This historical approach to landscape continues up to the present day, but there has also been some degree of separation.

That separation was most visibly portrayed by Aston in 1985, when he set out his approach to interpreting the landscape. This placed the emphasis on archaeology and on aerial photographs, but saw the contribution of history largely through 'documents which give good topographical detail, such as manorial court rolls, surveys and extents'. However it was the dismissal of the rest of the history that seemed to me to signal the establishment of a non-local history approach: 'the stock-in-trade of many local historians – genealogical material, parish registers, and the mass of nineteenth-century documentation – tends, on the other hand, to be of very limited interest to those involved in the study of the history of the landscape'.[5] It might be reading too much into this to suggest that local history and landscape archaeology had by then parted company, but I suspect most local historians will feel uncomfortable at the thought that their 'stock-in-trade' sources don't allow them to engage in landscape history. In reality, these very sources are extremely useful for tracking property descriptions in medieval and early post-medieval documents through to the present day, although the methods involved would justify a book on the subject. Too often archaeologists are just guessing the locations in medieval documents, whereas better use of historical sources would ensure accuracy.

The geography of local history

Part of the problem, however, is the extent to which 'the locality', as distinct from 'local', influences how local historians approach their subject matter. How much does the place where local history happens – in terms of topography and spatial relationships – influence the outcome of a local history project? The physical evidence of the past was seen as part of local history in the 1970s. Stephens' *Sources for English Local History* (1973) is an early handbook for the local historian, and recognises that 'the study of topography will necessarily involve fieldwork and the physical examination of the existing landscape and townscape'.[6] His evidence includes 'the survival of earthworks and of ridge and furrow, the lines taken by streets, paths and waterways, and the botanical composition of hedges', and refers the reader to Hoskins and Beresford. A close contemporary, Alan Rogers, in his *Approaches to Local History* recognised 'two quite distinct, though related, senses' of the term history: both description of the past and reconstruction that arises from this.[7] Reconstruction often involves an understanding of place.

One of the challenges of local history is how to make a connection with the geography of the past. This in part depends upon whether the emphasis is on social or topographic history, but as Rogers pointed out these are co-dependent.[8] So, while a socially based history might avoid the geography of the past, it cannot escape being influenced by it. The past also shapes later geographies in some ways, and influences the subsequent geography of the place where those social processes took place. All local historians are, to some extent, concerned with places, however these places were different from today. The geography of today might have been shaped by history, but is mostly a representation of present needs and practices. The argument raised by the landscape historians was that 'the landscape is a palimpsest on to which each generation inscribes its own impressions and removes some of the marks of earlier generations. Constructions of one age are often overlain, modified or eased by the work of another.'[9] The analogy made is to old writing on a parchment, which is partly erased so that fresh writing can be inscribed over it, though traces of the previous use may still be discernable. It is a great metaphor, and in some contexts, such as medieval townscapes, it has validity, but mostly it is far from being that simple; past land-use patterns were often very different. This is because the rapid progress in social structures, economies and technologies in the last two hundred years have totally obliterated the motivations and purposes of people in the past.

The problem is how to make the connection with the landscape of the period being written about. Of course modern geography is not without clues. But, while some place names and features have a known antiquity, others are relatively modern names or features with a relatively recent history that have superseded the earlier topography. So often the sense of place is too much determined by the modern and recent landscape, and too little by anything that really connects with the past. An added problem is that past local histories, such as those by Victorian or Edwardian writers, used the geography of the time when they were written, using the commonplace of the time, that was meaningful to the intended readers. Often the places referred to are identified by the names of contemporary residents, like Smith's mill or Mr Brown's house, or by a house name like The Willows that has long since disappeared (along with the willows in question), or even archaic place names that have not survived to the present. Where several successive historians have written, they have tried, each in turn, to give meaning to these locations, ending up with a very confusing topography. The result for the present-day local historian is a collection of puzzles and incomplete patterns.

There are, of course, ways round this, such as old maps and plans, documentary material in archives or the local studies room of a library, or through local genealogy societies that are able to provide, as a spin-off from their main objectives, useful topographic information. There may also be some archaeological material available, such as more recent artefacts in a museum, found in a ploughed field or by a metal detectorist, or found in someone's attic, or the results of excavations, that provide a thread of evidence back in time. One other resource lies in surviving surface evidence of the past, such as foundations of buildings, patterns of enclosures, trackways and other residues of older landscapes, that can be used to make sense of the information in old maps and old accounts.

Nothing ever happened here

The inspiration for this chapter came from several short articles written more than twenty years ago in an archaeological newsletter called *Scottish Archaeological Gazette*, published by the Council for Scottish Archaeology. One published in 1984 was entitled 'History on the Ground',[10] while the second, published two years later was called 'Nothing Ever Happened Here'.[11] They represent two sides of the same coin. The puzzle for all local historians is to find something to write about. The answer may in part be to look at the landscape for clues. But the ability to search the landscape needs inspiration from the history. Otherwise where do you look? Of course, as we shall see, there are ways of setting about looking, but there needs to be a feeling that there is something to look for. One fieldwork method which we will encounter in Chapter Two is systematic survey, which entails walking in transects at regular intervals to record surface remains as features, but which is also applied to detecting artefacts (flints, pottery, coins) in ploughed fields. This is more likely to answer the questions posed by archaeologists. For the historian fieldwork exploration offers solutions to the historical quest, sometimes resolving a very localised problem, and structured surveys intended to cover the whole landscape are too remote from local history needs. This is perhaps another reason why local history and landscape archaeology parted company.

The 1984 article 'History on the Ground' refers to the discovery and interpretation of remains of the past. By the 1970s there was some criticism of traditional ways of doing this. The argument against it was that each participant, coming from different backgrounds and abilities, saw things differently, so the results, it was claimed, could not be reliable. This subjectivity was seen as justification of systematic methods of fieldwork, where no interpretation was attempted; merely recording features based on organised transects. It was argued at that time that there were more archaeological sites than could ever be excavated. Also, it was considered that air photo archaeology had largely rendered manual interpretation obsolete. That set the pattern from the 1970s, with most archaeological recording relying on crop marks in aerial photographs and a smaller contribution from systematic surveys. What my article tried to do was defend traditional interpretative fieldwork, particularly by local societies and individuals, on the grounds that, besides utilising local knowledge, participants could make repeated visits at intervals, to record change, including damage of known remains and the chance revelation of new. The article also tried to make a case for a more helpful atmosphere, because local history-based fieldwork was not supported by the archaeology mainstream, as expressed in the following paragraph:

> The task of recording and monitoring history on the ground is best tackled by local societies. However, there must be a conducive environment for all such activities, providing facilities for discussion, learning, and above all publication of field observations, even if these must remain as opinions rather than statements of fact. If the need for such research is one day recognised, there will undoubtedly be enormous regret at the quantity of individual effort in the past, which was never recorded in print, or at least received very restricted summary publication. At the present time, archaeological journals do not allow the publication of detailed descriptions of surface features, unless a substantial portion of the work included excavation. If surface observation and interpretation is not deemed to be archaeology, do we discard a great quantity of our archaeological heritage as being beyond the pale?

What should local historians be looking for?

The dilemma in fieldwork is whether to record archaeologically classifiable features, or to try to understand the landscape and any remains of the past, in order to better understand local history. No-one willingly chooses obscurity, which the latter approach could entail. However, for local historians, assessing the story within the landscape is part of the goal. What local historians want to learn from fieldwork is whether a farm or a manor house existed, and where it stood. They want to know whether the boundaries of an estate or a deer park are still visible, or whether there was really a Roman road where tradition suggests. This kind of fieldwork seeks to understand the setting of a local history. The purpose of such fieldwork isn't archaeological inventory, but greater understanding of the local landscape, and how it helps explain local history. Nevertheless most local historians would probably welcome the chance of making a key discovery, and the lure of discovery is a strong incentive to explore.

Understanding the landscape that influenced the history inevitably generates an in-depth understanding of that landscape, comparable perhaps to a gamekeeper, where the knowledge is about patterns of human activity rather than the habits of animals. This adds a further separation between archaeologically orientated and local history-based fieldwork. Most man-made features that can be discovered in a landscape have attributes that can be used to assist in detection. These attributes include topographical factors such as altitude, slope and aspect, which may be characteristic of places where other known examples have been found. It may be important for some features to be near a road or other routeway, close to a water supply, near good cultivable land, or in a defendable position. Therefore such fieldwork is informed by precepts of what to expect. This is quite at odds with the objective and systematic approach to landscape pursued by modern archaeologists, where it is perceived as essential not to have preconceived ideas about the landscape, and to approach it with an open mind. Such systematic approaches can be quantified for accounting purposes and standardised for consistency of results and uniformity of coverage. An archaeologist may be in a locality for a day or a week, and somewhere else the next, and perceives no need for an affinity with the landscape where the finds are made. Likewise the attributes such as location are added after the find is made, not used to make the find in the first place.

Perhaps the best way to develop this distinction is to look at an example of a fieldwork problem which can be approached both from an archaeological and a local history fieldwork standpoint. The example, which is revisited in Chapter Two, considers how a Roman road crossed a deep gully (Figure 1). The Roman road in question is Margary 703[12] which ran from the Roman fort at Ribchester (Bremetennacum) towards Kirkham in the Fylde, via Preston in Lancashire. A major obstacle between Ribchester and Preston is the deep gully known as Tun Brook, and the accompanying river cliffs southwards, including Red Scar, near the M6 on the east side of Preston (Plate 1). Tun Brook is about 23 metres deep where the Roman road is supposed to cross, with very steep valley sides. The brook joins the River Ribble at a bend where the river is diverted southwards. The combined obstacles extend over five kilometres from Grimsargh to Avenham Park in Preston, and probably influenced the layout of medieval Preston. A modern footpath, 300 metres north of the Roman road, presents walkers with a challenge, as they are more likely to find themselves sliding towards the footbridge than walking; the valley crests here are only 100 metres apart. Undoubtedly, as Tun Brook is eroding fairly soft sediments, the valley was much shallower in Roman times, but it must still have given the Roman engineers a headache, as the gully extends over a kilometre north of the crossing. Yet there are no traces of the bridge where it is supposed to cross Tun Brook, nor indeed are there any traces on the approach either side.

In archaeological terms, the course of the Roman road is known from recorded exposures and excavations, and the crossing of Tun Brook is an unverified course between verified sections, albeit several kilometres apart. The question of how the Romans crossed the gully is not therefore an issue; the road exists as an entity, which does not depend on finding evidence at Tun Brook. However, from a local studies point of view, Tun Brook presents an interesting problem, because it was an obstacle not only for the Romans, but for travellers through the ages, most of whom made the detour round the head of the gully, at the village of Grimsargh. About a kilometre south of the Roman road crossing, there is a slightly easier crossing on the Ribble Way, where the ravine is nearly 30 metres deep (Plate 2). There was also a steep road in the eighteenth century called Pope Lane, at the confluence with the Ribble, but there the ravine was over 40 metres deep, and it is hard to imagine anyone finding a route there today. In 1991 the writer decided to investigate whether the barrier had ever been bridged further north, and with the aid of several permits, as Tun Brook is an important nature reserve, carried out a survey along the length of the gully.[13]

This undertaking was goal-led and inquisitive rather than objective. The approach is not about archaeology, but an attempt to understand how a physical

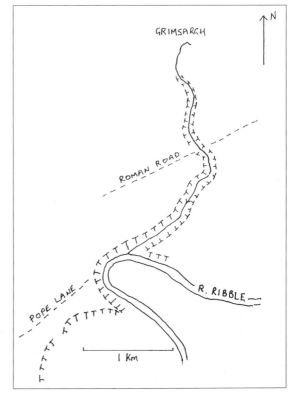

1 Tun Brook, near Preston and the Roman road crossing. The village of Grimsargh developed at the head of the valley, where most routeways avoided the obstacle, but the Romans seem to have crossed the gully. *Redrawn from a published map by permission of Ordnance Survey on behalf of HMSO © Crown copyright (2008) All rights reserved. Ordnance Survey Licence number 100048555.*

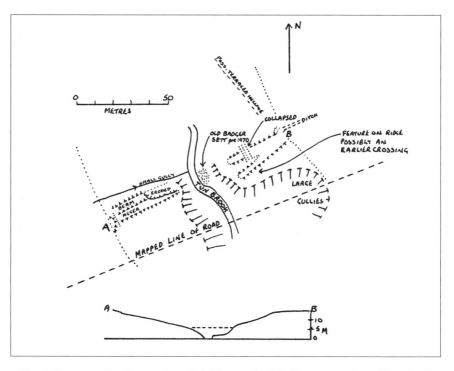

2 Sketch from 1991 showing remains of a bridge north of the Roman crossing of Tun Brook. Graded inclines and bridge abutments make better use of natural bluffs, whereas the mapped Roman Road line crosses steep, unrelenting valley sides.

barrier affected people in the past. Knowing this would be useful right across the timescale in a local history project from prehistoric to present day. To achieve this requires some understanding of the different ways that routeways can descend steep slopes, either by taking advantage of notches or small valleys through the escarpment or finding a gradual descent by a long detour or zig-zags. The approach uses knowledge, acquired or already available, to understand a problem that people would have had to address in the past – it is the 'gamekeeper' part of local history on the ground. At Tun Brook it was based on the assumptions that if the gully was crossed by a road at any time in the past there would still be traces. Possible clues included a recess or dip in the valley crest, banks or mounds on the sloping valley sides, or structures on the valley floor, that could have supported the superstructure for a wooden bridge or even a stone bridge. Therefore, whereas an archaeological survey might look systematically for further evidence of the road approaching on either side of the gully using air photographs, geophysical prospecting or excavation, the operating principle was that any crossing, at any time in history, would leave physical traces within the gully. The key distinction is that prior knowledge of how a road could cross a gully was used to predict the likelihood of a crossing.

After a number of visits, gradually working up the thickly vegetated valley floor and along the valley crests, only one feasible crossing point was found. This was only 20 to 50 metres north of the mapped Roman road crossing (Figure 2). It coincided with a field boundary on the west bank, 20 metres north of the Roman road, which was based on a broad stony bank. On both sides there was a dip in the crest of the valley descending the upper slopes. On the east bank there was a projecting spur from the valley side 50 metres north of the mapped line, so the crossing was at an angle to the axis of the Roman road. Built out of the slopes on either side were two steep-sided mounds which were the abutments for a wooden bridge, about six metres above the present valley floor. These showed signs of collapse and reconstruction suggesting several rebuilds over time.

The discovery of a crossing point so close to the Roman road does not mean that it was Roman. It would mean readjusting the alignment of the road for several kilometres east and west, and the mapped line of the Roman road has not been modified in the years since. However it does show that the obstacle presented by Tun Brook was surmounted at some time in the past, close to where the Romans crossed, if the remains were not those created by the Romans. The result of the investigation was a greater understanding of the effect Tun Brook had on the adjacent landscape in terms of communication between the areas either side. As such it contributes to a greater understanding of the local history. The archaeological perspective remains unchanged: the road is a fact – how it crossed Tun Brook is irrelevant (even finding road remains on the new alignment west and east of Tun Brook hasn't altered the archaeological perspective). One view is about understanding landscapes and how the people who lived there in the past coped with the constraints of their environment. The other is about classifying man-made objects and features within the landscape, and reflects the objectives of archaeologists. The former viewpoint is more likely to assist local historians.

What about the topographical history factor?

However, the other side of the coin was how to find out about the landscape from the history. Aston recognised the 'outstanding exception' provided by the Victoria County History series.[14] Structured around the old hundreds and their constituent parishes, the Victoria County History may seem a little intimidating to new users. Moreover, the mainstay of each parish history is the identification of the constituent manors, the genealogies of the owning families, and the history of the parish church, which only offer limited insight into topography. Both the VCH and its predecessors are excellently reviewed in a collective guide published in 1994.[15] However what the Victoria County History (VCH) has done, which sets it apart from earlier county histories, is to record as footnotes the documentary sources used. As such, the VCH provides a detailed synthesis of the information available in both published and manuscript sources, and this includes vital topographic information. To make full use of this, however, researchers need to follow up on the primary resources themselves. Scotland and Wales only have some county histories and other collectives. Scotland has the Old and New Statistical Accounts, produced respectively in the 1790s and 1840s, together with the Third Statistical Account in the 1950s, which record social, environmental and archaeological information.[16] Scotland also has collections of landed family estate papers and extracts of burgh records published by subscription societies in the nineteenth century.[17] A county-by-county programme of history volumes is underway in Wales.

The article 'Nothing Ever Happened Here' addressed resources for topographical information in Scotland. 'Perhaps the most daunting prospect for the amateur looking at local archaeology is to live in an area where nobody thinks there is a chance of success.' Many localities appear on the surface to have had little or no history, even though they may be surrounded by areas rich in history, but the apparent vacuum can merely be the result of the inequalities of previous researches. Alternatively the area had a history, but no trace of it survives, for such reasons as too much ironstone mining or very destructive intensive farming, where everything was ploughed flat years ago. Another variant is the area where everything has already been done; where 'everybody else has found everything there is to be found', such that any new venture cannot possibly add to existing knowledge. The trouble is, if you live in such an area, or want to study such an area, and want to make it the subject of a local history, such pre-judgements can be an obstacle to getting started, or having the confidence to persevere.

The surprising thing is that the wealth of material, particularly in property records and family estate papers, is seldom touched. For some reason it has never been seen as good history material, often consigned to the status of local history, and unattractive to scholars in consequence. Nor does much of it get utilised by landscape historians and archaeologists, whose resources are more specific, such as surveys and estate plans. However what it can provide, and what 'Nothing Ever Happened Here' tried to point out, is inspiration and a greater sense of place in the historical sense. Such sources can be used to reconstruct past geographies. For some inexplicable reason, it has largely been ignored, and the situation has changed little since the article was published more than twenty years ago. There are several possible reasons for this. Property-related material gives an incomplete picture, because so much evidence has not survived, and because the reference points described in the documents are no longer identifiable. Of course this is where the 'stock in trade' sources become very useful. Therefore it does not seem to assist scholarly activity except in very specialist spheres such as urban historical morphology (studying urban structures and layouts), histories of key properties, or detailed family histories. In such contexts, often confined to very precise localities, it is little surprising that there are large areas still offering opportunities for exploration. Similarly in landscape history, the aforementioned shortfalls make it less attractive and too time-consuming. However, for the local historian, the partial information such sources provide may be the difference between starting a productive project and abandoning one wrongly perceived to be fruitless.

This writer was inspired by an early experience of 'lost history' during production of a local history of his former home territory in the 1980s. Home, at the time of writing the book, was in Surrey and later Hampshire, but the locality in question had been the home base for the explorations and researches in the late 1960s and 1970s, that had provided the fuel for the book. Northwards it was a mile from Glasgow's city boundary, while a mile in any other direction led into five parishes, three in what was then Renfrewshire, and two in Lanarkshire, with a sixth parish a little over two miles distant. All these parishes had rich histories and contained the estates of well-documented landed families, and had also proved rich hunting grounds for fieldwork. Home itself, however, was in that part of Cathcart parish not absorbed into Glasgow by 1938. Cathcart too had a rich history, but Cathcart outside Glasgow just seemed to share Cathcart's history; it hadn't any history of its own. While I explored a rich heritage all around me, I seemed to be living in a historical vacuum. Yet, delving into some of the Scottish Record Office publications, notably the *Register of the Great Seal*, I suddenly found some perplexing topographical information that seemed to be saying it wasn't true. The trouble was, it was being described in connection with places a long way away, and for nearly a year, sometimes it seemed to be part of my immediate local history, and sometimes the idea fell apart as a new piece of information turned up and threw everything into disarray again.

The two main parts of the jigsaw were properties belonging to the Cochranes of Ascog, on the island of Bute, more than 50 kilometres west, and the Lekrevicks of Kilbride, seven kilometres south-east. In both cases some of the lands mentioned appeared, from the published transcriptions, to be in the main settlements being described, but were in fact in the parish of Cathcart. It was only after identifying a number of documents for these places that it became certain that Cathcart was the true location (see Chapter Three). By chance, Cathcart outside Glasgow was also outside the principal Barony of Cathcart, forming three small estates known as Cochrane's Lee, Maidlee and Cunninghame's Lee, together with several other small units that had their own histories. By fortunate coincidence, on Christmas Day 1984, while out walking in a local park half a mile from home, I had found in the roots of a recently fallen tree some three hundred sherds of pottery, dating from the thirteenth century to late medieval, mainly fourteenth century (Plate 3). This had been the site of a castle described in the New Statistical Account.[18] Within a year I had acquired the history of Cochrane's Lee from 1425 onwards, in previously uncharted territory, through a succession of owners, and with several mentions of the castle.[19] Home stood within Maidlee, which I was similarly able to document for the first time, from 1505 onwards, and which was usually described as lying between Cunninghame's Lee and Cochrane's Lee. Looking in Public Record Office volumes provided a local history of a place where 'Nothing Ever Happened Here' which otherwise might never have been conceived.

Local historians as custodians of their past

I have hinted at a third area to which local historians can contribute: monitoring change. This is outside the 'local history on the ground' theme, but not irrelevant to mention at this stage. In the 1984 article 'History on the Ground' I argued that one of the great advantages of local societies and individuals was that they regularly explored their local landscape. They are therefore best placed to observe changes or threats to known archaeological remains. This was very true of my home territory in the late 1960s and 1970s on the edge of Glasgow,

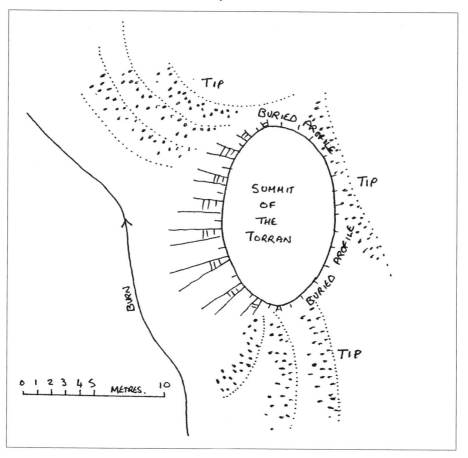

3 The Torran, near East Kilbride. This once free-standing motte castle had been mostly buried under landfill when the writer visited it in 1973; it illustrates the value of local historians keeping an eye on things. (Sketched 1973, redrawn 1982.)

as the city was expanding and archaeology was a hindrance to development. In one case in 1969 there was a motte in a small valley near Glasgow which the landowner was busily burying by offering the site for landfill (Figure 3). At the time I spotted what was happening, only the very top of the motte was showing through a jumble of broken porcelain and bricks.[20] Another farmer was busy filling in a medieval ditch.

Sometimes the developments can reveal information. Particularly remote areas tend to suffer from treasure hunters, intent on finding buried treasure or other claims in local legend, having the advantage that their targets are seldom visited by archaeologists. So a succession of visits to a site will often show up progressive despoliation. Occasionally though the treasure hunters uncover something new. In 1970 I visited a small fortification in Sutherland in north-west Scotland, An Dunan at Kylesku. This was on a tidal islet close to the shore and had been supposed to be a simple dun, having a very thick drystone wall in proportion to

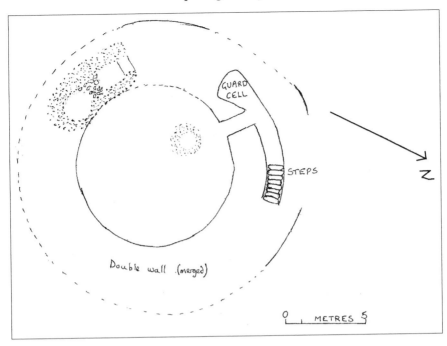

4 An Dunan, Kylesku, Sutherland; sketch made by the writer in 1970 to record changes (see also Plate 4).

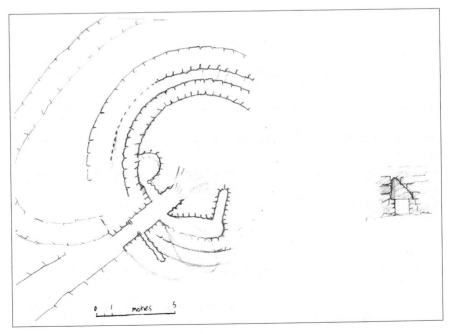

5 Broch at Clachtoll, Sutherland; sketch of passages made in 1971, at same time as interior photograph (Plate 5).

quite a small internal area, but no obvious structural features. It seems the previous year a holidaymaker had spent the duration of his visit moving stones around and eventually uncovering the wall structure. This included a passage between inner and outer components of the wall, leading from the inside of the dun to a flight of eight steps up to the present crown of the wall, and in another direction to a small chamber within the wall thickness (Figure 4 & Plate 4). This had changed the classification from dun to broch, the latter being a tapering stone tower with passages and galleries within the wall thickness. I was the first informed visitor to An Dunan after this well-intentioned but not-to-be-encouraged amateur excavation had taken place, and was able to inform the right people.[21] There is also an archival role in gathering evidence over time, in case the opportunities are subsequently lost, through destruction or deterioration of remains. Plate 5 shows the interior of another broch at Clachtoll, 18 kilometres west of An Dunan, photographed by the writer in 1971, but no longer feasible due to subsequent collapse of some of the passages (Figure 5).

Sadly the potential for local history societies and local archaeological societies to monitor local archaeology has never really been widely achieved. The creation of county archaeology units made this a professional role, and although the professionals couldn't look at everything as often as local amateurs might do, amateur participation seems mostly to have been discouraged. Yet so much could have been done to record the disappearing past over the last three decades, had there been a more conducive environment. The monitoring role is marginal to the primary objectives of this book, as it is more archaeology than local history, but I thought it worth including in this introductory chapter as an added dimension.

This chapter has suggested that the separation between archaeologists and local historians came about because local history seemed not to serve the needs of archaeology, and the objectives and methods used by archaeologists to assess remains in the landscape seemed of little relevance to the needs of historians. However by changing the approach to fieldwork to one which allows the historian to engage with the landscape and resolve historical problems, fieldwork can once again play an important role in local history. The next four chapters explore the possibilities further, Chapter Two by examining how best to interpret landscapes through fieldwork, and Chapters Three and Five by looking at how documents can help to elucidate topography. Chapter Four looks more closely at how the surviving remains of the past should be assessed.

Chapter Two

THE LANDSCAPE DETECTIVE

In the first chapter I explained that local historians have different fieldwork objectives from archaeologists, and that this to some extent explains the different development of landscape history. The local historian needs to understand the landscape, and to engage with it. The archaeologist is more likely to be concerned with discovery and inventory of discrete sites, which need not involve either engagement with the landscape nor a deep understanding of it.

It can be a bit daunting for local historians. Having come across local traditions or documentary references that seem to explain the past occupation or use of a site, it doesn't make life easier to find that the archaeologists have classified it as belonging to a different period. Archaeological fieldworkers are looking for simple classifications in order to inventory the past, and don't want the complication of detail. Local history fieldworkers are trying to make sense of the historical record in relation to what can be seen on the ground. The two sides were never suited to work together. The author would like to see the development of a discipline mid-way between archaeology and local history where the two concepts could work to advantage, but that is probably material for another book. For the present the aim is to help the local historian explore local history on the ground.

How to read the landscape

What is surprisingly absent from most books, either on fieldwork or landscape archaeology is explanation of the actual process of reading the landscape. There is plenty about what evidence to look for, as Chapter Four explains, but with regards to the 'how?' factor, it is often taken for granted that the practitioner will know about this. As Aston and Rowley suggested, 'landscape fieldwork basically involves observing and recording mainly relict features with the aim of explaining the evolution of patterns and shapes in urban and rural landscapes',[1] while a decade later according to Aston, 'fieldwork at its most basic involves walking across the landscape recording features seen on the ground'.[2] Recording features amounts to classification and inventory, and marks the emerging distinction between archaeological and local history fieldwork. For the local historian the objective may be something less tangible than features, perhaps just a sense of how past peoples lived and worked within a landscape. But is just 'walking across the landscape' enough to achieve this?

Two books which have addressed the issue in more depth in the past are Aston and Rowley's *Landscape Archaeology* and Taylor's *Fieldwork in Medieval Archaeology*, both published in 1974.[3] The timing of both is significant, as from the mid 1970s archaeology took a more objective approach to fieldwork, and a greater dependence on air photo archaeology. Aston and Rowley explained the need for a coming together of a wide range of skills, only some of which the individual fieldworker can possess, therefore necessitating some caution, and 'only patience and practice will give the field-worker an appreciation of all these skills, though he can soon develop an eye for patterns and features of particular interest'.[4] However the need to acquire skills through patience and experience can sometimes be a bit off-putting to those who have other objectives only partly served by fieldwork. Moreover, it was being recognised thirty years ago that differences in skill and background led to differences in the quality of fieldwork, and this was considered too unreliable a method for archaeological inventory.

Christopher Taylor's *Fieldwork in Medieval Archaeology* remains an invaluable book, and is mainly on surveying earthworks, but giving guidance on interpretation and reconnaissance. Chapter Two is concerned with discovering sites in the field, and contains some very good advice, such as 'the importance of walking over and around sites cannot be stressed too much' and 'a field visit still gives an appreciation of the physical setting that no map or photograph can ever do'. Another, often forgotten, piece of advice is that 'slight undulations of the surface … can often be of great significance'.[5] Taylor advises searches around existing monuments, visiting sites at different times of year over several years and in different conditions; the importance of winter fieldwork when ground cover is minimal; and monitoring of the processes of change in the landscape. He also makes the very valuable point that over time, with growing experience and local knowledge, features can be more accurately interpreted. Although the emphasis is still on finding features, Taylor provides more insight than most into the methods of finding.

A decade later two books appeared to address the landscape interpretation needs of the local historian, but both were written by archaeologists, primarily for archaeologists. These were Mick Aston's *Interpreting the Landscape – Landscape Archaeology and Local History* (1985) and Tony Brown's *Fieldwork for Archaeologists and Local Historians* (1987). The local history element was probably more in the subject matter than the methods. Brown was already advocating systematic survey by line walking, along the same lines as fieldwalking for artefacts. This approach is perhaps best represented in Drewett's *Field Archaeology: an Introduction* published in 1999.[6] Aston's book goes directly to the issue of interpreting earthworks and other evidence, without shedding any light on how to find them in the first place, other than 'basically observing and recording'.

How modern archaeologists read the landscape

Brown's *Fieldwork* gives considerable emphasis to 'fieldwalking', which at one time embraced any kind of reconnaissance in the field, but from the 1970s meant mainly systematic survey of ploughed fields looking for artefacts. In 1978 the Council for British Archaeology brought out a guide to this process aimed at a young audience together with sections on documentary research and aerial archaeology.[7] There was a flurry of fieldwalking activity in the 1970s and 1980s which made a very important contribution to our understanding of spatial patterns of past human activity. By plotting distributions of pottery, flints, metalworking and other objects disturbed by the plough or the harrow, many more archaeological sites were identified. It had the limitation that it was only practical on fields then undergoing ploughing, so areas with more permanent grassland than ploughed fields did not benefit so much. This may also have brought about a downturn in popularity of fieldwalking, as the numbers of areas left to cover diminished, but it should be kept up wherever new land is brought under the plough, or in case changes in ploughing practice brings new evidence to light in areas previously mapped.

Fieldwalking relies on volunteer enthusiasts who are willing to work in cold and damp fields as well as sunny ones, as overcast conditions after rain provide optimum conditions for detection.[7] Sometimes there are few finds to be made over large areas, while a few fields may prove very productive. The fields are traversed in parallel lines, on an eyes-down basis, looking for artefacts that contrast well with the soil or the stones in the soil, so it depends on a practiced eye and acquired skill. Finds are labelled and bagged and find spots marked so their exact positions can be recorded. Some of the best fieldwalking seems to have been done by small groups of experienced enthusiasts. However it has also been offered as a means for local people or amateurs to participate in archaeology, where the participants may find it harder to develop the skill or sustain the enthusiasm, especially if they feel exploited rather than involved in the outcome. Participants have not always got as much from the experience as the archaeologists running the programmes, and it depends greatly on good mentors and participation in the results. Some local history or archaeological societies have made important contributions to knowledge of their areas through fieldwalking. Local historians may find fieldwalking a useful resource, both following up on previous activity, which is not always well published, or engaging in some fieldwalking themselves.

However, as already mentioned, a development of fieldwalking which local historians are likely to encounter is systematic survey for remains and earthworks. Whereas fieldwalking for artefacts records distributions of small objects, which would be difficult to achieve by any other means, the use of the same format purely to produce lists of surface features rather takes both the skill and the engagement with landscape out of survey. This kind of fieldwalking has been offered as a means of amateur participation in archaeology, and is sometimes taught in archaeological certificates offered by adult education centres. As a means of producing inventories of features in the landscape it can be very effective and many people have found it a useful way of engaging in archaeology, especially where there is a good supporting infrastructure. It may be much less beneficial to local historians, however, as it doesn't engage in an understanding of the landscape. The intention is to impose an artificial framework for the collection of evidence. This reduces the impact of differing skills levels, subjectivity or differing levels of thoroughness incurred by more interpretative approaches.

Areas are divided into grid squares searched individually, or are traversed in parallel transects. Each landscape feature, whether a bump or a ridge, or standing remains, is recorded as an object. The resulting list includes piles of stones or bricks, gateposts, a track or wall crossing the line, or a grassed-over structure. The distribution of features generated may then be interpreted by a professional archaeologist to identify meaningful constituents and patterns, although the participants themselves can be the experts who rationalize the list. Ideally the transects should be in two directions, perhaps at different times of the day, and especially on sloping ground, where what you see walking downhill is very different from walking uphill. With such precautions, there is a good chance that every detectable aspect of the landscape will be recorded, but the local historian may find this acquisitive approach much less rewarding than an inquisitive one.

However, interpretative fieldwork, based on getting to know the landscape, may be actively discouraged by archaeological organisations. Because modern archaeology insists on classifying features and making inventories, they seek ways of making survey quantifiable and uniform. Interpretative fieldwork very much depends on the natural abilities of individuals and the skills they acquire, and is also influenced by any preconceptions or biases each individual may have. No two interpretative fieldworkers see the same things. So objective fieldwork – systematically recording feature entities or fieldwalking ploughed fields looking for artefacts – is mostly what is on offer to amateur archaeologists. Amateurs who insist on being landscape interpreters in their own right may find themselves shunned by professionals and professional-run societies. This makes it quite tough for local historians, whose primary need for fieldwork is better understanding of the landscape, and thus a very subjective and individual approach.

How to find out what has already been found in your area

The local historian may be fortunate in having recognisable and readily classifiable antiquities in the project area, however the chances are these will already be known. So it is important, first of all, to find out what other people have reported in your project area and what they have written about the remains. The obvious place to start is the local Historical Environment Record (HER), formerly known as a Sites and Monuments Record (SMR). Consulting an HER can provide an inventory of what is already known in the project area, including upstanding remains, low profile remains, sites where remains formerly existed, and artefacts found, together with other people's descriptions, or directions where to find these. HERs are usually maintained at county level, or several former counties defined as a region, but sometimes more locally, as records for a town or a district within a county.

The accessibility of HERs can vary: some are only accessible by appointment, even though the records, such as a former card index, may have been partly computerised, so that you can find the main details of a site at a terminal and then look at more detailed paper reports and photographs. Some are already on the web, or have more restricted access through a central library terminal. Local historians and amateur archaeologists up until a decade ago had to sit for hours transcribing information from card indexes; nowadays you can probably get a printout for a small fee. Progressively web access to HERs is becoming the norm, but the quality is still very variable. Some provide little more information than was formerly provided by a card index, while others have links to plans and photographs, as well as published texts. With the poorer web-based HERs it may still be necessary to visit a central depository to look at hard copy, although sometimes, for a small fee, photocopies may be supplied by post. National databases are also being realised, such as CANMORE in Scotland, although at the time of writing the English equivalent was still under development.

If there is or has been an active county, town or district archaeological society which covers your project area, they may have compiled their own archaeological record. For example, while researching Edward I's lost town of Gotowre-super-Mare (see p32), I used the Dorset Archaeology Society archives in Dorchester Museum, which included transcripts of the Public Record Office calendars relevant to Dorset together with manuscript sources. If the society publishes a journal or other periodical, this may contain similar but less well structured information, such as articles on specific sites, or past surveys of a locality. Some journals provide a means of summary publication of fieldwork within the timescale of each issue, perhaps a year or several years, from which you can determine who has done fieldwork in your project area in the past, and what they saw. A similar resource may be available from a Regional Group of the Council for British Archaeology, most of which publish an annual report of fieldwork and excavations in their area. In either case, by working back though previous issues, a picture of fieldwork activity, or lack of it, in your project area, can be built up, and knowledge gained, if not of antiquities within your project area, across a wider area. When using such resources, take into account fieldwalking evidence, which provides distribution of artefacts of a given period, crop marks found from air photographs, reports of artefacts handed into museums, and the results of excavations. All such information helps to build up a picture of what might be expected in your project area.

There may be a published inventory covering your area such as the County volumes of the Royal Commission (in England now part of English Heritage). The older inventories prior to 1950 tend to cover just the monuments already recorded, but more recent inventories attempted some fieldwork to find new earthworks, although mostly they just reported crop marks and evidence for artefacts from fieldwalking. Since the 1980s there has been a shift towards understanding landscapes rather than mere inventories, although the result is much the same. These landscape evaluations are broken down into feature classifications, which are itemised, and their patterns of distribution and a few best examples discussed. Lastly, so much of the country is affected by new roads, pipelines, pylon routes, windfarms or major afforestation programmes, it is likely that there has been fieldwork along the proposed corridor, or a survey of the affected area. Sometimes these are published, but others may have to be accessed by private arrangement with the contractor or the local Historic Environment Record.

Fieldwork for local historians

This book advocates a very different approach to fieldwork from the methods favoured by modern archaeology. The reader, in all probability, just wants to understand the historic landscape better, and to try to find evidence on the ground for things mentioned in documents, or to find evidence that fills gaps the documents cannot supply. Hence local history on the ground is about getting to know your home territory and building up an in-depth understanding of what can be found. If the reader does want to make new discoveries, rather than just be a local historian, hopefully the advice in this book will help to make that possible.

　Before you can actually find remains you need a process through which to organise finding. Modern archaeologists have their grids and transects. What the local historian needs is some sort of direction on how to walk through the landscape and how to observe effectively. As an analogy, dog walkers don't see much wildlife, because as the dog bounds through the undergrowth barking and sniffing around, and the owner shouts after it, usually ineffectively, any wildlife with any sense gets well out of the way. That doesn't stop some ecologists taking the dog along for company, but they are attuned to what to see, and it is the landscape and the life within it that has their full attention. Likewise the local historian needs to develop a sense of what to look out for, and how best to move through the landscape in order to best see what might be hidden there. What you need are some questions to ask yourself about aspects of the landscape to help lead you to the points of interest. One really useful landscape feature to start with is a valley, as this is both a barrier to communications (steep banks, crossing water and boggy ground) and a resource (water supply and water-power).

　In Chapter One we looked at the Roman Road crossing of Tun Brook, near Preston in Lancashire. On one hand there is an archaeological element to this: finding out how the Roman road crossed a deep gully. However there is a wider issue, which is how the deep gully affected communications and the relationships between settlements right through history. Settlement developed at its north end, at the village of Grimsargh. The contemporary landscape either side is agricultural, and may have been so in the past. However, Tun Brook offers something less likely to be thought of today, which is security and defence. If you cannot cross the brook other than by long detours, you can at least partly defend a settlement alongside it, especially where the gully bends or a deeply incised tributary forms a promontory. The more open aspects could be defended by a ditch and/or a bank. So the ground either side of the gully could also be explored for signs of early defended settlements.

However there are other things you could look for in a valley. Tun Brook is fairly small and not viable for water supply or to power a mill, and the narrow confines provide little prospect of a millpond. But in larger valleys with greater streamflow and occasional remission in the valley confines, a water mill might be expected to have existed at some time in the past, which would require a steeply inclined path as a means of access. Tun Brook has a very narrow floor that twists and turns, and is difficult to follow on foot, but a larger valley might provide a route for foot or horse traffic in one direction, up or down the valley, when in other directions, such as across the valley, it is a barrier. In another situation we might look for routes accessing the valley floor on one side only, which would give a clue to some past activity on the valley floor. This line of questioning has shifted the Tun Brook exploration from how the Romans crossed it, to how it fitted into human activity over time, from prehistoric to the present. We are now interpreting the landscape rather than recording archaeological features.

This is an inquisitive approach to landscapes, although a different use of the term as advocated by Bowden.[8] Whereas fieldwalking for surface patterns aims to reduce subjectivity by superimposing an artificial structure on the process, this inquisitive approach engages with the landscape and tries to understand how it might have served or hindered people in the past. In Chapter Four we will explore this inquisitive approach in terms of observed features, but for the present the objective is familiarisation and interpretation of a landscape's potential. It is similar, perhaps, to how settlers in the past, from prehistoric to present day, would have approached the landscape to see how best to use its resources. It anticipates how they would have organised their settlement infrastructure: places to live, communication routes, places to protect livestock, places of defence, sources of water, food, fuel and clothing and building materials. Sometimes the easiest way to pose appropriate and meaningful questions is to try to view the landscape from an early settler's perspective, and that means understanding something about their needs and concerns. That may mean reading up on the social and economic characteristics of past peoples through histories, reconstructions and theoretical studies.

The second part of the process is how to move through the countryside in order to ask these questions and make these deductions. We are not concerned with making an inventory here, so systematic coverage of all the ground is not an issue. What would be more effective for local historians is to select routes through the countryside that give the best opportunities to pose the aforementioned questions. The route can be meandering, via existing paths or safe routes, and can accommodate detours and local sorties aside from the main scheme of things. Again this is an inquisitive approach to landscape. It might take in key vantage points, or explore facets of the landscape that offer the best opportunities to interpret both the presence or absence of patterns of land use that might offer clues to the past. At its simplest this means going for a walk along a route that provides the best opportunities to appreciate diverse surroundings. And this is perhaps also what early settlers did in the past to size up this landscape.

The questions suggested here are not prescriptive and do not need to be applied exhaustively. The objective is to increase awareness of the constraints and benefits of different landscapes and to approach each landscape inquisitively. Whether writing a local history or giving talks to local societies, such fieldwork will enable the historian to communicate convincingly about the landscape in question, and engage their audience's interest and imagination. A good way of developing this skill is to visit well-known archaeological sites or monuments, especially if they have been discussed in books, papers and guides. Look at each site visited in terms of how it fits into the landscape, what the landscape constraints and benefits are, how it relates to communications, water supply, security and defence. If good archaeological practice has been followed, the site should have been assessed with these characteristics in mind, so it should be possible to compare your own impressions with those of experts. This will inform your own landscape investigations and make exploration stimulating and worthwhile. However we will come back to these questions when we begin to look at the evidence itself, in Chapter Four.

Maps and air photographs

Two items that can facilitate this exploration are good maps and vertical air photographs, which are covered in Chapter Five. The ideal Ordnance Survey scale for local history fieldwork is 1:25,000 (2.5 inches to the mile). These show topographical details found at the next scale up (1:10,000 or 6 inches to the mile approximately) on a portable folded map sheet covering an adequate area to explore. There will always be some areas that lie on the edges of maps, and if there is no overlap two maps may have to be carried, and rarely as many as four. The First and Second Series editions, now obsolete, revealed an area 20 kilometres east to west by 10 kilometres, usually based on two ten-by-ten kilometre squares. The new Explorer Series usually provide in excess of 20 kilometres east to west by 30 kilometres north to south. The detail on these maps includes most field boundaries, accurate woodland boundaries, paths and tracks, and water features including small streams. These are basic needs for navigation. The next scale down, 1:50,000, currently known as the Landranger Series, seldom shows field boundaries, and graphic representation is just at the level where accuracy becomes difficult (a line half a millimetre thick on the map, whether a boundary or a line in text, represents 25 metres on the ground, and this has the effect of cluttering the map). The next scale above 1:25,000 is 1:10,000 which will show not all that much greater detail, but covers much less ground on a portable sheet (5 x 5 km). On maps at this scale it is easier to give accurate grid-references and to plot the courses of tracks or linear earthworks. However for detailed mapping work much larger scales are needed, which would only accommodate very small areas of ground, e.g. one kilometre square.

It is important to understand how to read and use grid references. A six-digit reference is used to define an area 100 metres square which contains the referenced site. The reference identifies the south-west corner of this square so the referenced item could be up to 99 metres east or north of that point, and more like 120 metres north-east. Because of this 8 digits or better are usually sought, but are quite hard to achieve accurately by conventional means, and offsets from two or three mapped landmarks are essential. Eight digits defines the south-west corner of a space 10 metres square. It is important to give Eastings before Northings ('along the hall then up the stair'), as these are often given the wrong way round. Nowadays GPS seems to prevail, but few seem to understand the resolution and calibration issues. Five years ago Glasgow archaeologists were claiming my grid references from the 1970s in East Renfrewshire were consistently wrong. When I checked I found my alleged error was consistently in the same direction by the same amount, so I challenged the author of the rumour. He accepted there was a calibration error on his GPS but insisted it didn't account for all his alleged error; would I go 50/50 and accept part blame? He seemed not to comprehend that errors consistently in the same direction, besides the amount, were more likely to be system errors rather than human error. GPS coordinates should always be checked against a map.

Small-scale air photo coverage is now widely available, both on websites and as atlases. While this may not provide the detail available in the field, such photographs are very helpful in backing up the information on maps, and helping to plan routes. Some website air photo coverage will zoom in on larger scales. Many libraries now hold large area coverage of colour or black and white photographs at 1:10,000 scale or thereabouts, which can be used to look at the landscape in more detail. The value of air photographs will be developed in Chapter Five.

Access: asking permission

Though perhaps something that should have started this chapter, something needs to be said about access. It is always good practice to obtain permission before carrying out any fieldwork. On farm land it is not always possible to identify the authority who can grant permission; sometimes the farmer is an absentee and the nearest farmhouse is a private residence. Sometimes a tenant farmer will not be able to give permission without the landowner's consent, and sometimes land is owned by overseas investors or private companies only accessible through a land agent or solicitor. Woodland, river banks, and non-farming land such as landscaped parks can be very much harder. Sometimes awkward paperwork can appear, such as liability indemnification forms, an increasing obstacle as accident or personal injury litigation becomes an issue. This can often make the access process quite tricky, and the advantage of embarking on a local history is that usually the right procedures can be found out quickly.

Where finding out about who to ask for access is difficult, there is sometimes a temptation to go ahead anyway. But the historian is in a difficult position compared to the casual walker, if they intend to write about the area subsequently and have to explain how they got their information. Someone wandering around land looking as if they are searching for something can be a lot more worrying for farmers than a stray dog walker. So it is an important courtesy to seek permission first.

However, there are other benefits to sorting out access. Farmers and other landowners usually have useful knowledge about their own land. There may be things that puzzle them that might be worth looking at, or they may be able to provide simple explanations for features that puzzle you. I often ask farmers if there are any mystery features on their land or amongst their farm buildings I might be able to help explain. In particular, older farm buildings often retain details of past use, such as the vents or power take off for threshing engines, or horsepower and water-power driven machinery. They may have old plans or estate papers they are willing to show you, or they can direct you to where such papers have been deposited, or tell you whom to contact if someone has previously done research. It is also a good idea to let farmers know the outcome of any fieldwork or documentary research on their land. Farmers are likely purchasers of local history books, especially if these books pay attention to farming history as well as more conventional topics.

Questions to ask during fieldwork – a gateway into inquisitive exploration based on Edward I's lost new town in Dorset

By attempting to recreate past perceptions, the local historian is trying to understand the landscape in different ways from the present. While some roads and boundaries perpetuate patterns in the distant past, the way to understanding the historical landscape is to try to see beyond the present-day network of roads, fences and settlements. It is about trying to visualize how the landscape might have been. To explain how the local historian might approach the landscape, the following investigation carried out by this writer in 1988 used a town that never was, to work out where it might have stood.

The subject matter was Edward I's new town of Gotowre-super-Mare, planned, at least on paper, in 1286, somewhere on the southern shore of Poole Harbour on the Isle of Purbeck, in Dorset. This puzzle, though identified as far back as 1923, was first brought to public notice in 1955 by W.G. Hoskins and three years later by Beresford and St Joseph.[9] It was supposed that the site was at Newton, to the west of the Goathorn peninsula (see Ordnance Survey map Plate 6), because the town is referred to as Nova Villa (new town) in one document, even though documentary evidence suggests that the place name in this locality only dates back to the seventeenth century. In 1962 possible remains were identified on the east side of Goathorn.[10] This aspiration was dashed when analysis of timber in one of the foundations showed the site to be a seventeenth-century fishing settlement.[11] Instead, foundations excavated west of Newton at Ower in the late 1980s were subsequently identified as the only surviving remains of the town.[12]

Two documents survive which testify to the foundation of this town, one in January 1286 which tasks officials to set out the town, and a second four months later which grants the town the same rights as Lyme or Melcumbe and a weekly market and yearly fair. Thereafter there are no references to it. It has thus been deemed a failure, either because the harbour silted up or because it lost out to Poole, founded forty years earlier.[13] A more likely explanation is that the plan was overtaken by events. Even before market rights were granted Edward I was planning an expedition to Gascony, that was to last three years, and on 18 April

Richard de Bosco, the official tasked with laying out the new town, was sent there with the advanced party.[14] There may also have been a problem with land at Ower given to Milton Abbey by King Athelstan, title to which was confirmed in 1311.[15] Milton Abbey's land included a historic deep-water landing place, known as Ower Passage, which might have been crucial to the success of the planned town.

The debate hinges on whether Gotowre-super-Mare was a poorly chosen site that didn't prosper, or a carefully chosen site that was never actually taken beyond the planning stage. The writer's investigation focused on the latter possibility that Edward I, who knew Corfe well, had identified a site with good all round potential. Therefore, by looking at the landscape from King Edward's point of view, it might be possible to identify where he intended it to be built. If the location of Gotowre-super-Mare was well thought out, could the intended site be determined from its likely attributes? The founding charter tasked officials 'to lay out, with sufficient streets and lanes and adequate sites for a market and church and plots for merchants and others, a new town with a harbour.'

That gives us something to look for. We can search the landscape for sites that meet these attributes. The main landscape features (see Plate 6) are three peninsulas –Vitower, Ower and Goathorn, and the shores of the bays or inlets in between. We can go further and set up some criteria for finding any lost settlement, or investigating an existing settlement, which in turn provide us with questions to ask when exploring the landscape:

- Space to build
- Protection and defence
- Access and communications
- Water supply
- Land to farm

Space to build

For a viable medieval town you needed an area at least several hundred metres square. There needed to be a viable number of houses to provide sufficient income from rates to pay the duty to the Crown. These houses would occupy plots (known as burgages) of sufficient width, in these times of timber frame construction, for one or two bays or frames fronting the street, together with a passage to one side for access to the rear of the property. The house might extend five or six bays back from the street, followed by outbuildings including workshops and storage for trade, and open space for outdoor activity. The size of burgages varied, but 10 metres wide to the street and 60 metres in length would be fairly typical. If each of these paid four shillings (20 pence) rates a year, and the duty to the Crown was say £20, you might need a hundred burgages, although commercial rates for shops and larger manor houses would take up some of this amount. Adequate space for a market might be 100 metres square, and a church and churchyard might be up to 100 metres square as well. If you had just one street with 30 burgages each side, a market square, a church and a harbour area with warehouses you have easily got a town 300 by 300 metres in size. All three peninsulas – Goathorn, Ower and Vitower (see map on Plate 6) could have afforded sufficient space.

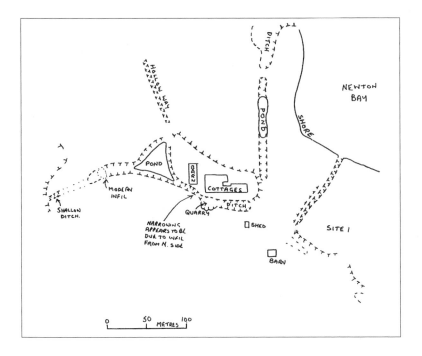

The following labels appear on the sketch map:

DITCH

NEWTON BAY

POND

SHORE

POND

BARN

COTTAGES

MODERN INFIL

SHALLOW DITCH.

DITCH

QUARRY

NARROWING APPEARS TO BE DUE TO INFIL FROM N. SIDE

SHED

SITE 1

BARN

0   50   100
METRES

6 Sketch of earthworks around Ower in Purbeck, Dorset, 1988, under permit from Rempstone Estates. Figure 9 shows the next area to the east.

Protection and defence

Besides building a wall around it, which would not necessarily have been attempted in the thirteenth century, there would need to be scope for a mix of natural and artificial defence. The need for defence was not only to keep out armies in times of war but to keep out smaller numbers of troublemakers on land and pirates at sea, as well as keeping out wild animals. Each of the peninsulas could rely on water or at least tidal mudflats for protection, with a wall or ditch across the neck of the peninsula. Vitower is perhaps best equipped as it has a cliff facing the landward, south side. Both Ower and Newton Bay are to some extent overlooked by rising ground to south. A further problem with Newton Bay, and Brand's Bay to the east, is that nowadays it is very shallow at high tide and mostly just mudflats, but Goathorn has a steep shore in places which could compensate. There are both earthworks and crop marks around Ower Peninsula (see Figures 6 and 9) if these can be differentiated from any down to Milton Abbey grange or post-medieval land management. Goathorn is currently dominated by scarps and hollow ways, mostly products of post-medieval activity (Figure 7) but nothing to suggest it was ever artificially defended.

Access and communications

The new town was meant to have a harbour, preferably deep water access, or at least space to draw up small boats used to unload larger ships in deeper water

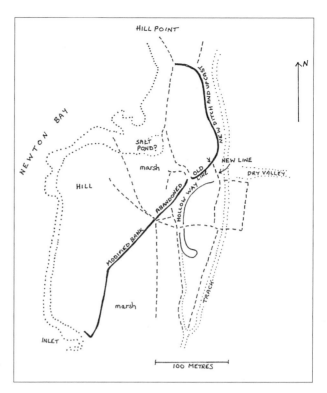

7 Sketch of mostly post-medieval features at Goathorn, Purbeck, 1988, which archaeologists previously supposed was the site of Edward I's new town.

offshore. Piers and jetties leading towards deeper water might be one possibility. Poole Harbour is the estuary of the rivers Frome and Piddle, which flow through the narrows of Wareham Channel, but it also takes in minor streams from north and south. Those to the south rise on the Purbeck Hills or the heathlands on their northern flank, and are very short and insignificant, with the exception of Corfe river, which draws on a number of small valleys south of the Purbeck Hills and flows through the gap at Corfe. The tidal inlets on the south side of Poole Harbour are very shallow, divided by islands and shoals. Most of the deep water flows around the northern part of the harbour, either side of Brownsea Island, and probably did so in medieval times, but there is a channel between the smaller islands known as South Deep. This currently provides deep water access from some points on the southern shores, particularly the north-western flank of Goathorn, Cleavel Point and Ower Passage, and the islands at Fitzworth (see Plate 6). The Claywell Brook flows between Vitower and Ower and may be a factor in maintaining deeper water at Ower Passage. There is an interesting inlet at Vitower (see Figure 8).

If the new town was intended to serve as a trading point there had to be good overland communications, not least with Corfe Castle five kilometres (three miles) south-west of Newton Bay. One interpretation was that it was intended to provide a landing place for supplies to the castle. Three successive monarchs had invested Corfe Castle, and Edward I had just completed construction of the outer bailey and gatehouse (National Trust booklet). The new town may well

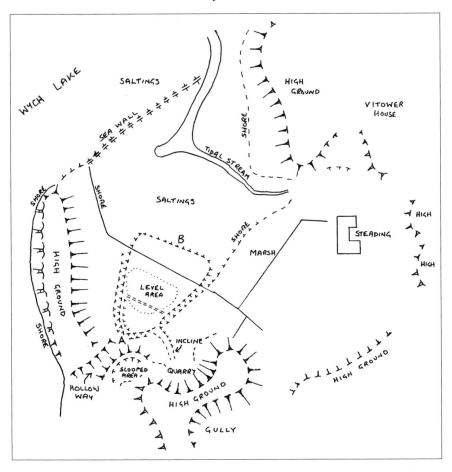

8 Sketch of features around a former inlet at Vitower, Purbeck in 1988. The inlet closed by a recent embankment is now a saltmarsh and the triangular platform projects into the inlet to provide a quay. Access by permission of Rempstone Estates/Fitzworth.

have been under consideration for some time as a useful adjunct to the castle. Communications should therefore be capable of supporting carts or pack-horse traffic, and avoid the boggy land found along much of this coast. Equally the subsequent decline of Corfe Castle after Edward's reign might in part be attributed to the difficulty getting supplies to it. Routes would have had to cross Wytch Heath and Rempstone Heath, avoiding several tracts of boggy ground. The heathland south of Newton Bay and Goathorn is criss-crossed by post-medieval tracks, including several from the general direction of Corfe, but nearer the shore the route is crossed by several small east–west valleys and intervening ridges, which tend to isolate Newton Bay to this day. Although access has been further impeded by old clay pits developed along some of these valleys, the pre-existing terrain casts doubt on the claim that the site of the town was destroyed by the clayworkings. Ower and Fitzworth are better placed than Newton and Goathorn in terms of access from Corfe.

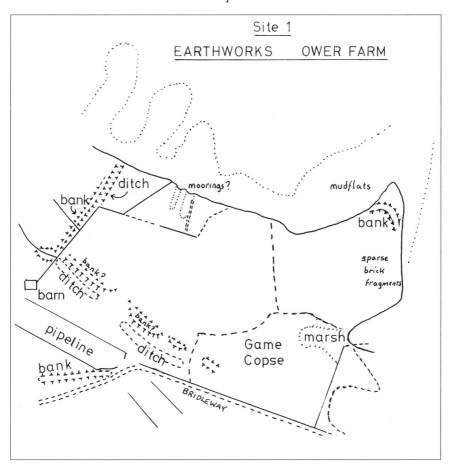

9 Sketch of earthworks east of Ower Farm, Purbeck in 1988. These lie to the east of those in Figure 6.

Water supply

There had to be a supply of fresh water, either from wells or springs, which close to a sea inlet could become contaminated by brackish water if resources were overdrawn. This means sufficient water to supply the needs of a town, both to drink and to engage in produce such as brewing. Both Newton and Goathorn have a limited water supply today, having a high risk of brackish wells through overdrawing. The Vitower peninsula, lying between the tidal reaches of streams, also has a lack of potable water, but the land sloping towards the inlets east and west could provide both well water and stream water. The Ower peninsula is the most likely location to afford good water supplies to a town.

Land to farm

Much of the area nowadays is heathland, with small cultivable areas near the shore. Things might have been easier in the thirteenth century. The town would need agricultural land within reasonable reach of the town, and the means to irrigate it. The Ower peninsula appears to offer the best agricultural land.

From this simple breakdown it should be possible to locate Edward I's intended New Town in the present-day landscape. In fact the problem was resolved by careful use of the topographical information in the documents, and we will revisit this in Chapter Three.

However what this chapter proposes is that local historians begin to think strategically and practically about the landscape they are exploring, and the process of posing questions will help to determine where and how to look. In this strategy, local historians may find themselves at odds with archaeological practice, especially where there are active local archaeological societies or community archaeology projects led by professionals. However the needs of local historians are very different from those of archaeologists, and you should choose the fieldwork approach that best suits what you want to get out of doing it. If you want to understand the landscape, systematic approaches may not suit you. However some local historians may find objective survey more beneficial because it enables collaboration with archaeology specialists.

Chapter Three

THE LANDSCAPE HIDDEN
IN DOCUMENTS

My own interests began with fieldwork and the idea of combining this with local history came later. For most local historians the fieldwork develops from a primary interest in history, though hopefully it will one day become second nature to do both. It had never occurred to me that local history would help because, although I had read local history books to find ideas and inspiration, I could not find the answers to what I was puzzling over on the ground.

Also, for many years I was caught in the inventory trap, which just means recording lots of feature remains for the sake of doing so. While an undergraduate, my personal tutor in my first year edited a newsletter on industrial archaeology. He got me interested in recording industrial remains in my home area, such as watermills, water power on farms, lime kilns, and quarries. One year I trekked around every farm across three or four parishes, recording horse engine houses and mill rinks or horse gins, or even just the traces of where they had been. These are horse-powered engines used for threshers, butter churns and pumping water on farms, and consist of a circular walkway for the horses, either in the open or within a building that allowed the horses to work in all weathers. Talking to the older farmers who remembered how these worked, and searching farm records and old maps, built up an interest in the history as well as the remains. Often, however, I just did surveys that produced lists of remains, which after a while felt lacklustre and routine.

My next opportunities to make more use of local history came with my interest in Roman roads (see Chapter Seven), when I realised I needed to back up my impressions on the ground with thorough documentary research, both manuscripts and old maps and plans. Then two events revolutionised my thinking. In 1983 I was invited to write a local history of the area south of Glasgow that was my early inspiration, so as to record for posterity my archaeological adventures in a historical context. Then in April the following year I changed jobs and moved to Titchfield, near Fareham, in Hampshire. There I joined the Titchfield Local History Society. This industrious group had already produced one local history

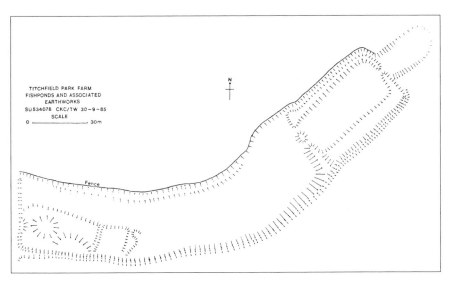

TITCHFIELD PARK FARM
FISHPONDS AND ASSOCIATED
EARTHWORKS
SU 534078 CKC/TW 30-9-85
SCALE
0 ————— 30m

N

Fence

10 Fishponds near Titchfield. This plan by myself and Chris Currie was originally published in *Hampshire Field Club Newsletter* New Series 6, Autumn 1986 p18–19.

volume collectively, and had embarked on a second.[2] I went on a training visit to the Record Office in Winchester, where members were introduced to early documents. I also met the late Chris Currie, an independent archaeological consultant who was interested in fish ponds and gardens. At the time he was excavating a medieval monastic fish pond at Titchfield Abbey (Plates 7 & 8), one of the few occasions when I have joined a dig, though just to push a wheelbarrow around. Chris introduced me to the idea that documentary research could greatly enhance my fieldwork, and helped me to follow up and publish some monastic fish ponds I discovered using old maps and documents combined with fieldwork (Figure 10). The long curving upper pond on the left has several platforms, possibly for a drying house, while the better preserved east pond has a stone-lined by-pass channel on the north side, very typical of a monastic fish pond.

After a year I joined the committee of the society, and contributed to the second volume of their local history project, just before work moved me to Christchurch in Dorset. I owe a tremendous debt to what I learned from one thriving and adventurous local history society in Hampshire. In 1986 I began another important collaboration with Dr Stuart Nisbet in Glasgow, mainly on industrial archaeology, at first helping to expand the industrial content of my first book published in 1989. Subsequently we jointly wrote a book on Greenbank Estate near Glasgow (Robert Allason and Greenbank) in 1992. Both of us combine fieldwork with documentary research, and the collaboration greatly enlarged my knowledge of historical sources.

Topographical sources

There is not the scope in this book to go into detail about the range and location of historical documents, which is well represented in books on local history, including such classics as Tate's *The Parish Chest* and West's *Village Records*.[3] Rather, this is an opportunity to say something about sources that provide useful clues to help understand the landscape. Chapter Two introduced the value of posing questions and looking for answers in the landscape. Documentary research to that end should perhaps be approached in the same way, by posing a series of questions. Apart from searching in Record Offices one of the first resources I found useful, and continue to use whenever possible, are Public Record Office volumes such as the Calendars of Patent Rolls, Charter Rolls, Close Rolls, Fine Rolls, Coram Rege Rolls and Inquisitions, notably Inquisitions post-mortem, as well as their Scottish counterparts, such as the Register of the Great Seal. Most of these volumes have indexes that include place names. Printed volumes of family histories, for the great landed families, often include abstracts of charters. Records Societies have contributed greatly, in some parts of the country, in providing similar resources, and most County Record Offices have good place name indexes.

The Public Record Office calendars can be found in larger public libraries, as well as university libraries and museums. They are usually much neglected and poorly cared for, because they take up a lot of space and appear to get little used (I often find copies where most of the pages are still joined at the edges), and even in active local history rooms are amongst the least used of resources. In consequence they are kept in damp basements or in side rooms and corridors, where the bindings fall apart and the pages turn brown and crumble. Occasionally a library will restock with new editions, but it is not uncommon to find them tied together with string, or kept in a box, because they have become so fragile. These are among the sources so familiar to historians who start their explorations with the Victoria County History (VCH), lost in the small print in the footnotes. In the VCH they are searched and collated to provide genealogies of the key land-owning families and to trace the history of the constituent manors in a parish, or the history of a county town. However, occasionally the footnotes indulge the reader with tantalising glimpses of topographical information, such as furlong names, names of streams or woodland.

Public Record Office Calendars are often a good way to start looking for topographical information. As a way in, you need first of all to make a list of likely place names or surnames to search for in the index. You need to go back to early Ordnance Survey editions, or eighteenth- and nineteenth-century county maps, or older estate maps (see Chapter Five). Older names may turn up in the process, making it necessary to go back through the volumes already covered. The same applies to manuscript sources in county and national record offices, where there is a place index, as well as in published family histories or in Records Society volumes. Sometimes the index to manuscript sources includes an abstract, and sometimes these provide topographical information, or will at least indicate whether the document contains such information. The distinction in record office archives is that you may be able to find more topographical detail further back in time than the published calendars, where the printed extracts are less concerned with local detail. Where there are no place indexes, the process will be much slower, and will need more research to identify workable clues such as names of owners. Occasionally there is no alternative but to work through the documents themselves.

However you also need to be able to locate these topographical clues on the modern map. Sometimes the documents contain sufficient information, such as a stream, or a road of verifiable antiquity, or a parish boundary, or a landmark that survives to the present day. More often the information is meaningless in modern contexts, including other properties equally hard to place, roads that have long since disappeared, and transient landmarks such as vanished woodland. So you need information to help you connect the past with the present. This is where the 'mass of nineteenth-century documentation' can prove very useful. Sometimes place names continue to be used in legal documents long after they have ceased to be used in common parlance or shown on maps. Because of the difficulties in describing a piece of land sufficiently to avoid dispute, documents recite earlier descriptions, including old names and the succession of tenure of both the property and the neighbours, so that at some point, even if only a few decades or a century removed, it can be linked in with something placeable. Even where this doesn't extend near enough to the present to place it, it can be tracked down though nineteenth-century documentation such as rate books, rentals, mortgages, property transfers, wills, genealogies and parish records. It is sometimes possible to establish a timelink, like a borehole through time that enables something described on thirteenth-century documents to be placed in present-day contexts.

Questions to consider during topographic research

There are very sound reasons why local historians should resort to topographical information in documentary sources in the course of fieldwork.

1 Looking for obvious explanations
2 Reconstructing past geographies
3 Checking other writers' interpretations of past geographies
4 Changed landmarks
5 Identifying the commonplace in past writings
6 Past land management

1. Looking for obvious explanations

What the local historian is trying to achieve through fieldwork is a better understanding of the landscape so as to convey this to the readers of a book, or members of an audience. Part of this task involves finding, interpreting and explaining remains, which will be explored in Chapter Four. The problem with this is that, depending on how many reliable clues can be found, the fieldworker is employing a best guess, based sometimes on experience, or comparison with known remains of similar character. But that interpretation could add erroneous 'history' to the landscape. It would be good to be able to explain all remains of the past with confidence, but there is seldom enough information around either physically or documented, to achieve this ideal. For example small cairns found on unimproved ground can have various interpretations such as places of burial or simply stones removed from the soil and placed in piles, in an unsuccessful attempt to cultivate (clearance cairns). The explanation might well be documented, such as mention of an attempt to farm there.

This writer had an early lesson in the importance of checking for obvious explanations some thirty years ago. I had found several circular platforms in a local park (Overlee, Plate 9), part cut into the slope and part built out, with a central depression filled with gravelly material. This seemed to relate to the discovery at Overlee about 1820, in the course of stripping ground for a quarry, of forty-two 'weems' or underground houses, thirty-six arranged around the slopes of a small swelling hill, and six in a circle higher up.[4] Each was part cut into the slope and part built out, and featured a sunken chamber or storage pit, drystone lined and floored with slabs, eight to twelve feet square and four to five feet high. All of these had been destroyed at the time, leaving it to subsequent historians to speculate what they were. The park had been created from the farm where this discovery took place. I thought I had found a couple of survivors and published the find in the publication *Discovery and Excavation in Scotland* in 1973. Two years later, in the 1975 edition, two local schoolchildren had published the revelation that one of my platforms was depicted on the 1912 edition of the Ordnance Survey 25 inch to the mile plan as a mineshaft, though the other platform was not so identified. I went to the library and dug out a copy of the plan, and sure enough there were two shafts depicted, one exactly where I had described my platform, the other, with some buildings, labelled Overlee Colliery. This second shaft was no longer visible but in the goal mouth of a football pitch. The mine had been a short-lived venture that had not appeared on the earliest Ordnance Survey editions, but only in 1912. After that I made sure that I checked all available old maps for more recent explanations of my finds.

2. Reconstructing past geographies

Before modern maps were available to record boundaries, a property had to be defined by means of landmarks or sometimes by describing all the neighbouring properties around its boundaries. However, while the landmarks may have been permanent enough at the time the property was defined, some may not have survived to the present day. As a consequence historians are presented with a challenge to identify the location described. This could be achieved by finding a document that describes the property in question, but as the examples given below demonstrate, the information can be tantalising. However it is also possible to locate a property from its neighbours, if their boundaries give clues, especially if a neighbour is indicated in the description. Sometimes the only recourse is exclusion, by finding out if anything else has been located in the expected place, or by finding a number of unconnected properties round about, sufficient to say roughly where it was. If the property had any permanence, such as land with a function or an ownership history, either the property sought or a neighbour may be traced through to more recent documents, amongst which there might be fortuitous evidence such as a ground plan or a more detailed description, or by which time early rate books, street directories or other community documentation might help.

As we have seen, Public Record Office volumes often contain useful topographic clues, and the following example comes from the Scottish series, the Register of the Great Seal, which helped to find the Bishop's Palace and fifteenth- century castle site at Dunkeld (Plates 9 and 10), 12 miles north of Perth. Here the post-Reformation documents record many of the prebendiary manses around the cathedral, by then in the hands of secular owners, originally provided by each parish to accommodate cathedral canons. Each of these is described with its neighbours north, south, east and west, to provide a historical jigsaw puzzle. There are enough clues to identify the present High Street as 'Scottisraw', and to locate key buildings, such as the Earl of Atholl's house east of the cathedral. West of the cathedral ruins, one of the manses was north of the Bishop's Garden and 'lie Muthill', possibly signifying the motte on which the fifteenth-century castle stood. This fitted in with references to the Bishop's Palace being south-west of the cathedral. Bishop's Hill to the west of this, although much altered by eighteenth and nineteenth century landscaping, shows evidence of being scarped as a motte, and there are traces of buildings on the summit. Prior to finding this documentary evidence what little was recorded was impossible to interpret, and the palace had been surmised to have been further north.

In Chapter One, I described the experience of discovering a medieval estate in home territory on the south side of Glasgow that had never been described by previous writers. My initial problem lay with a description in documents that contained familiar names, but was tied up with another property, on the island of Bute in the Firth of Clyde, 50 kilometres west. I had found these amongst charter extracts accompanying a history of the Montgomeries, Earls of Eglinton, published in 1859 where that family had acquired the lands of the Cochranes of Lee and Ascog (in Bute) in 1503, through the latter falling into debt to the Earl.[5] The key documents were in a batch of deeds for Lee and Ascog back to 1425. What these documents described was the northern half of the lands of Overlee (see Figure 11) which was occupied by Alice Cochrane, Lady of Netherlee, in 1425. Overlee and Netherlee are modern place names in the part of the parish of Cathcart not absorbed into Glasgow in 1938. Previous writers had assumed that this part of the parish of Cathcart lay within the main manorial property, the Barony of Cathcart. However, all previous research I could find had placed Cochrane's Lee in Bute, and I shelved the idea.

The turning point came with the discovery of another adjoining small division of Cathcart, known as Maidlee, which is described in 1505 as lying between Cochranelee and Cunninghamelee.[6] This belonged to a family in the next county,

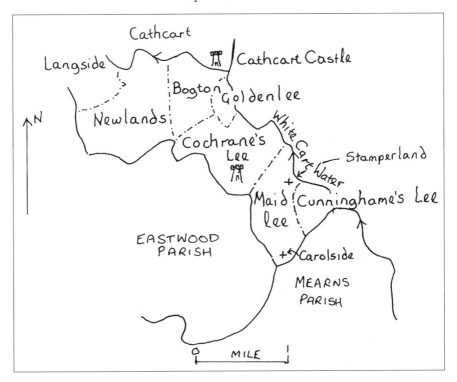

11 Map of Lee names in Cathcart Parish near Glasgow, to show the relative locations of Cochrane's Lee, Maidlee and Cunningham's Lee.

Lanarkshire, in the parish of East Kilbride, about eight kilometres south-east, and Maidlee had previously been identified as part of that small estate, now built over in modern East Kilbride. Their records had also survived after being obliged to sell to a branch of the Cunninghame family, Earls of Glencairn, who already held Cunninghamlee. What was curious about Maidlee was that it too contained place names similar to modern counterparts, such as Stawpartislandis (resembling the modern Stamperland) and Dedecarlside (resembling the modern Carolside, see Figure 11). Two estates with recognisable place names, particularly one with unusual place names, was harder to discount. However both estates could be followed through the records of their sixteenth- and seventeenth-century owners, and their successors up to the present day. Once the connection through adjacency had been established, two places once thought to be 60 kilometres apart could be brought together into one neighbourhood, by pursuing a sequence of records previously overlooked. Also, with research around the previously ascribed localities, it could be demonstrated that they had never been there, as there were quite different estate histories roundabout.

The following example also comes from the writer's original home territory. It typifies the mystery of so many early property descriptions. However it was also part of the land held by a church as part of its income up until recent times, and mentions a neighbour within its bounds that can be traced up to the twentieth century as a precise landmark. This is a charter for just under nine acres of land at Mearnskirk in East Renfrewshire, Scotland (10 kilometres south-south-west of the centre of Glasgow), dating from between 1272 and 1316 AD.[7] Translated from the Latin the boundaries are described as follows.[8]

> As the church rivulet crosses the highway that leads from the church of Mearns to the 'nova villa' and so up that rivulet northwards by that green furrow to the syke that extends westwards to another standing stone, and from that standing stone directly northwards to a rill at a well head, and by that rill by the well to Poddocford and thence by the highway to the place above mentioned where the church rivulet crosses the highway, excepting the land pertaining to the house of Thorphichen within these said boundaries.

The 'nova villa' might be present-day Newton Mearns; elsewhere the charter refers to the Aldton. The land concerned was a transfer of two pieces of land, described in comparable detail, from the Aldton to Mearnskirk, and probably

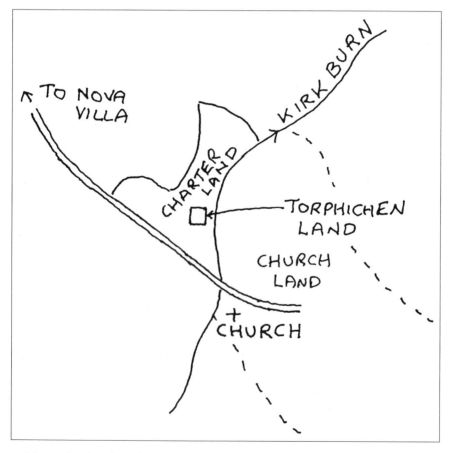

12 Mearns church and temple lands. Shows how the land boundaries of a charter of *c*.1300 can be resolved by looking for clues.

adjoined the other church lands there, so that at least the approximate location, within a larger church holding there, can be surmised. The church rivulet is probably the present-day Kirk Burn (see Figure 12), but the various rills, furrow, well and standing stone are unlikely to have survived to modern times. Scott, a retired minister writing in 1939 suggested that the land described was in the angle between the Kirk Burn and the road from Newton to Mearnskirk, and that a bend in the road there was still called Poddockford.[9] Seventy years on most of this ground is covered by modern housing estates, but the name Poddockford had been forgotten not long after Scott's day, and could not be found in contemporary documents. Moreover, Newton has moved several times in its history, such as when the turnpike shifted its centre from the old crossroads to the new, while in 1747 a local landowner diverted the road between Newton and Mearnskirk around his park, although it was restored to more or less its original line a century later. However, given the changes in recent centuries how certain is the identification of the highway to nova villa around 1300 with the modern road, let alone Scott's word of mouth identification of Poddockford, or even the identity of the church rivulet as Kirk Burn?

However the land pertaining to the house of Torphichen is identifiable; it concerns an acre of temple land which survived in documents up to the nineteenth century, and was still enclosed by a drystone wall up until the 1980s. In Scotland the lands confiscated from the dissolved order of Knights Templars in 1309 were given to the Knights Hospitallers and their lands were turned into secular holdings after the Reformation. Many of them can be traced to precise boundaries. Torpichen Priory was the principle seat of the Hospitallers in Scotland. There is a detailed documentary history of former Hospitaller holdings in Renfrewshire, and this particular acre of land survived in seisins (land transfer records) of leases of the land in question. As shown in Figure 12 it lies within a triangle of ground between the Kirk Burn and the present road between Mearnskirk and Newton Mearns. So Scott's surmise was accurate.

3. Checking other writers' interpretations of past geographies

Making sense of other people's geographies can be particularly challenging. This is not just a matter of recognising features from obscure names, but of understanding contemporary thinking about how to read topographic clues in documents and earlier histories. Otherwise, the historian is left to make the best sense of what his/her predecessors have written, perhaps adding more misunderstandings and topographical errors. Each successive historian has fewer remembered clues to work with, as folk memory is lost.

The previous example demonstrates the value of new evidence to corroborate deductions made by previous writers. Such deductions are not always so reliable, but more importantly it is good practice to re-examine the evidence rather than rely on other people's conjectures. Someone else's best guess from the evidence available to them, might have been using information not available now. Equally more information is sometimes available now than then, especially with so many resources accessible on the web and in library catalogues. However occasionally past writers, perhaps for fear of showing ignorance or in order to make their own theories work, have knowingly included wrong or imaginary evidence, or failed to mention evidence that contradicts their theories. Sometimes it is just for the very simplest of reasons that searching around the subject would have taken too long, and a wild guess is passed off as fact. The local historian has a duty to at least contribute more insight than previous researchers or to make it known if the evidence is far from certain.

Sometimes this can be achieved by reviewing the known documents, and looking for new leads. To return to Gotowre-super-Mare; when I did my fieldwork in 1988 I only knew about the documents that previous writers had used, principally the founding charter. Previous writers had only described one piece of land, in the parish of Studland – 'in a place called Gotowre super Mare in Studland parish', 'the name of Goathorn peninsula is generally acknowledged to be a memory of Gotowre' and 'Nova Villa seems always to have remained in Studland Parish, where Edward instructed that the new town should be prepared.' There were in fact five topographic elements to the founding charter.[10] It was at a place called Gotowre-super-Mare, in the parish of Studland, and also on adjoining ground in the King's hands, that had lately belonged to Robert de Muchegros. That is, two adjacent land units are described, and one is not necessarily in Studland. I did not fully appreciate this until 1992, and it was not until 1998 that I discovered in the Calendar of Patent Rolls for 1281–92 that de Muchegros land lay on the warren of Corfe, and had been purchased for the use of the King by Richard de Bosco.

One can only guess why only one piece of land in Studland is mentioned by successive writers, but it is not uncommon for people to refer to a source they have not seen while relying on a previous writer's interpretation. Even though nowadays the printed Patent Roll volume is readily accessible in most large libraries, and is probably more accessible than the journals and out of print books they consulted, it is astonishing how often one writer relies on the accuracy of a predecessor rather than going to the primary source. Consequently, at the time, I had been confused because I knew that de Muchegros had no land in Studland, because there had long been a dispute over Studland in which de Muchegros was not one of the rival parties. At his death in 1281, an inquisition showed he only held lands in Berkshire and Rutland, even though it is recorded that he secured a loan on a property in Dorset in 1277, which was probably the land later acquired for the King.[11]

When I came back to this research a decade later, I tried a new tack: I tried to find out about the two officials appointed to lay out the town, Richard de Bosco and Walter de Marisco. The latter was parson of the church of Bromesburrowe, and a letter to the post office there secured me a copy of the church history (which I might nowadays have got directly from the internet). This revealed that de Bosco was patron of the church of Bromsburrowe at the time. Richard de Bosco was Constable of Corfe Castle at least between 1280 and 1299, and seems to have been in close service to the King. Within three months of the founding charter de Bosco was sent ahead of the King's party to prepare for the Gascony campaign, where King Edward spent the next three years, and in 1287 de Bosco was back in England as a sheriff's officer. It was through following the life of de Bosco that I found the earlier acquisition of land of late Robert de Muscegro in Corfe warren, which was on the south shore of Poole Harbour in the north-east corner of Corfe Castle Parish, that de Bosco bought for the King's use. Thus checking all the available evidence, and following up different aspects of the evidence, the key topographical clue was uncovered. The part of the new town site adjoining another part in Studland was in the adjoining parish of Corfe.

This placed the town on the boundary between Studland and Corfe parishes, at the mouth of the Claywell Brook, where the place name Shotover Moor provides something of a clue (Plate 6). Shotover is just a soft consonant version of Gotowre, and the 'on sea' may have been to distinguish it from the forest of Shotover in Oxfordshire, frequently mentioned in documents around this time (certainly it fits Gotowre better than Goathorn). The present parish boundary between Corfe and Studland includes the Ower peninsula, from a point on the Claywell Brook a kilometre south of the inlet, and striking east then north-east to follow one of the small streams into Newton Bay. This might have been a consequence of the two pieces of land continuing long after the failed town as one element in Corfe Parish. The moral of the story is always to look at primary sources and look closely; don't rely on intermediate writers.

4. Changed landmarks

Landmarks are seldom as permanent as we might suppose, because in documents they survive as descriptions of the landmark, which we may erroneously assume to be the same as something we recognise today. Worse the landmark may be of a very temporary nature such as a clump of thorn bushes or an old oak tree, or as we saw in the case of the Mearns charters, lost standing stones or wells. In reality the landmark may be no more than a place name or the briefest description. Often we can do little more than hazard a guess as to what they represent. Place names frequently change location, and a particular culprit is the transposition of place names in modern housing estates. In the eighteenth and nineteenth centuries place names were sometimes transposed from one estate to another, so that the owner could have familiar names around him at either place of residence. But the commoner process is simply that when a house or other structure is rebuilt in a different location, the name travels with it. Inn and public house names are a particular area for caution. Popular pub names transpose when a previous holder closes or adopts a new name, and another publican somewhere else takes advantage of the unclaimed name. However even where pub names stay in the same location, they sometimes denote pairs of adjoining houses, one of which is residential, and switch around when one or other house required renovation.

A simple illustration of this is a prehistoric burial cairn I found in 1979 at West Revoch, near Eaglesham, East Renfrewshire (Plate 12). It was shown as a cairn on the highest point on a plan of the farm by John Ainslie in 1789, but by the time of a later plan in 1834, the boundaries had changed, bringing in a higher piece of land

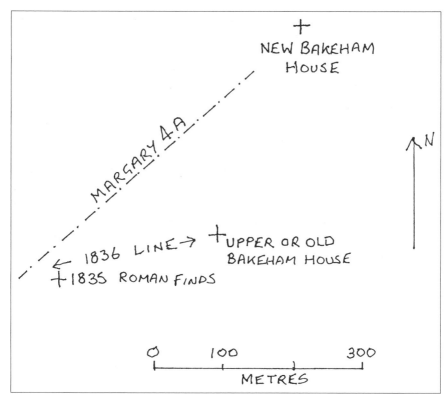

13 Old and New Bakeham House. Landmarks can change. This shows how Margary aligned his version of the Devil's Highway Roman Road to new Bakeham House, relocated in the mid-nineteenth century, whereas previous authorities had found the road towards the original Upper Bakeham House, 300 metres south.

called Garret Law. Garret Law also has faint traces of a cairn, which was thought for a time to be the West Revoch cairn. In the late eighteenth and early nineteenth century known cairns were ready targets for treasure hunters, or merely as quarries for stone for drains or road metalling. However the original cairn survives on a lower hilltop 20 metres in diameter, and despite quarrying into it, still standing up to one metre high, with the sides revetted in stone to achieve a conical profile.[12] This sort of change is very common as the next two items reveal.

Chapter Seven looks at the theme of Roman Roads, which are a characteristic subject that can crop up in any local history, but are fraught with interpretation problems. An example occurs for the Roman road from London to Silchester (Margary 4a), known as the Devil's Highway where it crosses the heathlands between Staines and Crowthorne.[13] The course of the road was first surveyed in the 1820s by engineering officers at the Royal Military College, Sandhurst, as a training exercise. In their description the road was found 'at Bakeham House, situated in the same line of direction.'[14] Bakeham House stood about 300 metres south-west of Royal Holloway College, near Egham, and is approximately where the Roman road is now believed to change direction from its steady

south-westward course from London. Thomas Codrington's account of the
Roman Road in 1903 is based on that of the Royal Miltary College surveyors,
but he noticed that Bakeham House was now called Upper Bakeham House
(Figure 13).[15] This was because a new Bakeham House had been built further
north, and the old house renamed. When Margary described the road in 1955, he
placed it at the new location of Bakeham House (Figure 13).[16]

There is another example of landmark relocation further west along the Devil's
Highway, where it passes between Bracknell in Berkshire and Bagshot, near
Camberley in Surrey. In 1773 a Berkshire farmer named Rapley levelled a banked
and ditched enclosure while reclaiming land from the heath, at a spot known
as 'The Roundabout'. The enclosure had become overgrown with thorns and
briars. The ditch, according to Mr Rapley, had been deep enough to take in a
road wagon. When this was subsequently ploughed, pottery was revealed, and
in 1783 an archaeologist, T.B. Handasyd of Hurst, recovered fifty vessels which
he illustrated in a paper in *Archaeologia*.[17] They included a cremation urn, jugs,
flagons, bowls and dishes and at least one mortaria. Ever since that discovery

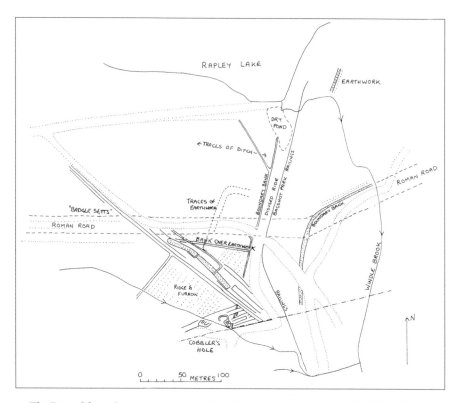

14 The Roundabout Roman site near Bagshot, Surrey, sketchplan from 1982. While following
a different course for the Roman Road called Devil's Highway, on a Crown Estate Permit, the
writer found pottery in animal burrows and fallen trees, which appears to indicate a Roman
settlement last described in 1783. The original site of Rapley Farm was at Heatly Bottom
or Cobbler's Hole, where there are remains of buildings and cultivation ridges. The present
Rapley Farm is 700 metres north.

many people have tried to find the site, including an attempt to dig up the farmyard of Rapley's Farm in the 1970s. What was not realised however is that the original farm, known as Heatly Farm, had been taken into Bagshot Park in the early nineteenth century, and was near Rapley Lake (Plates 13 and 14), and in compensation Mr Rapley had been given new land further north. The modern Rapley Farm is not near the original. The actual site was found by taking advantage of fallen tree roots and the casts from animal burrows, which revealed a range of Roman pottery (Figure 14).

Even quite large settlements change their location, such as when a new road route replaces an older one, as when the turnpikes were introduced in the eighteenth century, or where canals or railways passed closeby, and the centre of the settlement shifted to take advantage of the interface. Another Scottish example is Scone, to the north-east of Perth, traditionally supposed to have been a Royal City, though perhaps never more than a large village, which contained an important abbey. An early capital of Scotland, up until the end of the fifteenth century the Kings of Scotland were crowned there, and in keeping with tradition Charles II had an additional crowning at Scone in 1651. By the eighteenth century it had been laid out as a planned village east of the mansion house built on or near the site of the Abbey by the Earl of Mansfield, but this in turn was removed at the beginning of the nineteenth century to enlarge the park (Plate 15). In 1926 the site of the planned village – until then shown on Ordnance Survey maps as 'Site of the Royal City of Scone' – was relegated to 'site of the Ancient Village of Scone'.[18]

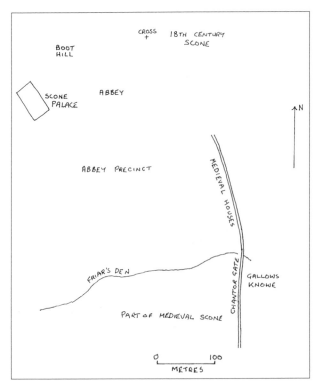

15 Scone, Perth. It has traditionally been supposed that the ancient Scone was on the site of the eighteenth-century model village, north-east of Scone Palace, but analysis of sixteenth-century documents shows it was around Gallows Knowe, on both banks of Friar's Den.

What no one seemed to have noticed, however, was a series of lease confirmations, mainly in Volume V of the Scottish Record Office printed calendar known as the Register of the Great Seal and dating from the 1580s.[19] When Scone Abbey was dissolved at the Reformation about 1560, its lands were originally granted to the Ruthven family, as Earls of Gowrie, who held it up to 1584 when that family rebelled against the King. Some of the houses and gardens in Scone that had belonged to the abbey had continued to be held by their occupiers on long leases or feus which had been disputed by the Earl. So at the forfeiture of Gowrie these claimants came forward with their records of leasehold title to protect their interests. What is intriguing about these leases is that they describe a town that was centred around Gallow's Knowe, on both banks of the stream called Friar's Den, and extended up to 300 metres south of the eighteenth-century planned village.[20] Ancient Scone was somewhere else (Figure 15).

As well as changes in the position of man-made features, changes to the natural landscape, such as coastal erosion undermining cliffs or washing away a coastal settlement, changes in the courses of rivers, or the draining of water bodies and creation of new ones, can affect how we interpret the landscape. Features in the modern landscape that were once underwater are more likely to post-date the draining of a small lake or pond, unless they represent defensive structures such as crannogs that were purposefully put there. Much more simply, deep ploughing and improvement in the latter half of the twentieth century has smoothed out numerous landscapes that had interesting features in the past. Some of this might be documented, particularly on old estate maps or in land management records, while wartime air photographs and earlier landscape photography can reveal what has been lost, but for the most part it will require observation to anticipate where topographical changes have occurred, backed by research into likely available sources of clues. Research using written records, as well as old maps and plans discussed in Chapter Five, may help to elucidate such changes.

5. Identifying the commonplace in past writings

It is important to fully understand the geographies used by previous writers such as past local historians. For example, as we have seen in Chapter One, they will have used names for places that were commonplace to their contemporaries, such as Smith's Mill. At the time it would have been named after the miller of the day, long forgotten, with the mill, if it survives today, under a different name, and if there is more than one possible mill involved, recovering the geography is that much harder. So it is important to fill in the gaps that previous writers thought they did not need to explain to their readers. However we have also seen how past writers have speculated about the geographies of their predecessors, and about the meaning and significance of topographical information in documents. It is essential to check out the validity of these earlier deductions. From one writer to the next, differing perspectives, including a different spin on events, will over time create erroneous and fictional geographies that need to be understood. Wherever possible topographical information in documents should be reviewed afresh,

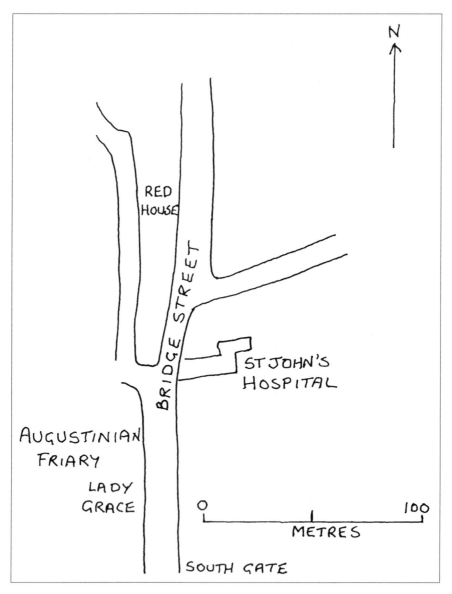

16 Finding Mr Painter's House, Bridge Street, Northampton. Locations of Lady Grace, Augustinian Friary and Red House, as clues needed to resolve an eighteenth-century commonplace.

rather than repeated from other people's deductions, lest these are in error, but to do that the available evidence of the past needs to be identified and explored.

Most previous historians wrote in the nineteenth and twentieth century, and for those times there are sources that can be used to identify commonplace references. Apart from old maps, which will be explored in Chapter Five, the historian has recourse to trade directories, rate books, valuation rolls and the census record books which, from 1851, as the 1841 census lacks detail, makes it possible to analyse street layouts in detail. This task is easier in the larger towns than in smaller centres and rural areas. From about 1860 the trade directories for towns began to record the occupants in individual streets sequentially, whereas in more rural locations such information was lacking until the twentieth century, with only trades and prominent gentry listed, often without clear locational details. Similarly rural rate books and census entries are less clear about local geography, but there is still enough information, with a bit of perseverance, such as by following through an ownership succession, to build a geography around commonplace information.

With earlier historians, their commonplace is both more distant and more elusive, but clues may be found on old estate maps (see Chapter Five) or a search of documents, if there are available indexes in libraries or record offices. Henry Lee, a former Town Clerk of Northampton, writing his history of the town about 1716, says 'There was also a Church on the West side of Lady Grace where old Mr Painter dwelt. It was formerly a Nunnery. I remember the walls and great windows of the Church still standing.'[21] It is not clear whether Lee was referring to the church of the Augustinian Friary, called Lady Grace, or a building which belonged to the nunnery at Delapre Abbey, but more than a century and a half after the dissolution its purpose may already have been forgotten. However neither the location of Lady Grace nor Mr Painter's house survived into modern times, although the approximate position of the friary is known, on the west side of Bridge Street. However in 1675 Northampton was largely destroyed by a fire. The commission set up to resolve disputes during the rebuilding of the town locates the house formerly occupied by Henry Painter as the Red House, below the inn formerly known as the Lyon and Lamb, which can be accurately positioned from other documents.[22] This may not be the same one as was next to Lady Grace in Lee's time. Documents survive in Northamptonshire Record Office which show that Henry Painter had formerly been the owner of the ground on which the Augustinian Friary stood, so he could have lived at Lady Grace.[23] Topographical evidence in documents can make more sense of local history on the ground (Figure 16).

6. Past land management

It is sometimes advantageous to know the organisation and layout of land in the past, as this may account for missing evidence or help find evidence. This includes the pre-enclosure organisation of land into strips grouped together in furlongs, information which can sometimes be gleaned from a study of old estate and enclosure plans (see Chapter Five) and sometimes from documents that describe the allocation of these strips amongst the farming community. Understanding where the furlongs were, and how they related to one another, with the assistance of air photographs and modern maps, can help to identify old routeways, and lost settlements and manor houses. Alternatively understanding the division of estates may be useful in understanding the origins of present-day farm names.

Topographical research amongst documents is a useful way to bridge the gap between local history and landscape history. It may help the latter to explore a greater range of local history research options. It may help local historians to venture into more fieldwork. What this documentary research does is to help to populate the landscape with an essence of the past, be that a manor house here or a mill there. Without the documentary research the fieldworker is exploring a blank canvas, where evidence found needs to be interpreted and understood in isolation, as will be explored in Chapter Four. The topographical research uncovers the possibilities. It provides questions to be posed and investigated. As Chapter Two explained, this may be subjective, and contrary to the archaeological precepts of objective detachment and systematic reconnaissance, but the local historian is not usually embarking on an inventory of antiquities. The local historian is trying unravel what happened in the past, and that needs to be based on an understanding of the landscape, not the detachment of an archaeologist. So in Chapter Four we go from exploring the landscape to explaining the remains of the past we find there.

Chapter Four

READING THE LANDSCAPE

An amazingly rich array of books is now available on structures and earthworks across history, all of which provide local historians with informative resources. These tell us about nearly every human-created landform we could anticipate finding, from rabbit warrens to fish ponds, from round homesteads to longhouses, from Roman temporary camps to deer parks, and from burial mounds to motte castles. Sometimes these are general explorations of landscape features by landscape historians, such as Richard Muir's books, including the most recent titles *The New Reading the Landscape – Fieldwork in Landscape History* in 2000 (University of Exeter Press) and *Be your own Landscape Detective – Investigating Where You Are* in 2007 (Sutton Publishing). Others are more archaeology driven and very specialist, such as *Inscribed Across the Landscape – the Cursus Enigma* by Roy Loveday (Tempus 2006) and *Rabbits, Warrens and Archaeology* by Tom Williamson (Tempus 2007). These resources provide local historians with a tremendous amount of information to help unravel the landscape they are exploring.

Finding out what to look for

The trouble with such thematic resources is that there never seem to enough subjects covered or enough attention given to how to find your own examples within any one subject. They do not always provide the sought-after solutions. There are three reasons for this:

- they are about categories of phenomena
- they often describe perfect examples
- they are often verified by investigative procedures that the local historian cannot readily emulate, like archaeological excavation

This is an archaeology-led approach. They tend to be about examples you can go to see. Going to see good examples is a useful exercise to help you develop experience in interpreting remains, however such books seldom explain how to find your own examples. Also the remains that local historians may encounter are incomplete, poorly preserved and less readily explained. Books about ideals do not tell us what to do if the remains we encounter are less than ideal.

Of more practical benefit are texts that focus on groups of key elements of the historical landscape. For example they may focus on the symbols of power in a landscape, such as castles, market places, major roads and monumental burial places. Others concentrate on the commonplace, such as field patterns, trackways and utility buildings such as farmhouses and mills. On the whole, the commonplace themes are more useful to local historians, because they deal with the nuts and bolts of most landscapes, while the high-status monuments, if not already on the map, are more likely to be hoped-for discoveries than readily attained. Richard Muir's *Be your own Landscape Detective* comes pretty close to fulfilling this need. Another book the writer has found useful is Susannah Wade Martins' *Farms and Fields* published by Batsford in 1995 (*Know the Landscape* series). Also there are several post-medieval archaeology resource books on the market, notably David Crossley's *Post-Medieval Archaeology in Britain* (Leicester University Press 1990). These multi-thematic books are good as first ports of call. Also useful is Stephen Friar's *The Sutton Companion to Local History* (2001), as it defines things you may encounter in the field.

Knowing what to find was not always as easily accessible as now. Back in the fifties, sixties and seventies the main resources were Collins' *Field Guide to Archaeology*, first published in 1963, and the Ordnance Survey's *Field Archaeology in Great Britain*, first published in 1921, and updated and enlarged in 1973. These differed from other books of the time by providing a comprehensive survey, across human timescales, of all the features likely to be seen, and the main identifying features to look out for. What they described however were the typical manifestations of ideal and well-preserved examples and the places where the best examples could be seen. They had something in common with the *I Spy* books that, in the same decades, encouraged children to look out for things on the road or railway journeys. Growing up in Scotland I found them immensely frustrating in that you had to live in the south of England to have any chance of ticking all the boxes in the book. The problem of regional bias and perfection of evidence has somehow determined the pattern for most landscape archaeology books since, in that they are mostly about archaeology rather than history. In order to make more effective use of these books, something has to be said about 'remains' and how to interpret them.

What was tantalising about Collins' *Field Guide to Archaeology* was the section headed 'Identifying Earthworks' which contained around twelve pages of earthwork types, each with ten to twenty possible explanations. This would tell you, for example, that oblong platforms could indicate a medieval deserted village, or a deserted church, or the site of a large house, or pillow mounds (rabbit warrens), or a bowling green, or an ornamental mount, depending on whether it was high or low or had a raised rim. But it quickly became obvious in practice that the list was illustrative, not prescriptive, and the range of possible explanations for oblong mounds was considerable. What eventually replaces having a guide book is accumulated experience of interpreting oblong mounds, gained at the cost of many mistakes and misunderstandings. However the local historian may not have time to become an expert in evaluating oblong mounds, so what is needed is a guide to the complexities and variations of oblong mounds. Sadly, a book on oblong mounds is less likely to catch on than a book about bowling greens or pillow mounds or medieval deserted villages, so the local historian is obliged to invest in many thematic books that still may not provide all the answers. The truth is we haven't moved very far from the archaeological feature-spotting of landscape archaeology books, because spotting whether a mound is oblong, round or star-shaped isn't providing all the answers.

So what's the secret?

'Reading the landscape' isn't just about the features to look for but how to interpret them in the context of a landscape perhaps with several different features present, belonging to different times. Archaeology texts tend to make this into a mystery by addressing the complexities and problems rather than explaining straightforward identification. One of the pioneering books in this field was Taylor's *Fieldwork in Medieval Archaeology* (Batsford, 1974). Chapter Four covers 'Interpretation in the Field' but is mostly concerned with what later writers such as Bowden refer to as 'stratigraphy in the landscape'.[1] Taylor gives various examples of the relationships between discrete archaeological remains and ridge-and-furrow patterns (the raised strips denoting pre-enclosure field systems). Some remains have been inserted into pre-existing ridge-and-furrow and are more recent, while in other cases the ridge-and-furrow was obstructed or diverted by remains which are older. However he demonstrates that decisions about which came first are often very difficult. Taylor progresses onto other stratigraphic relationships such as roads over or under moats, or later landscaping or adaptation of medieval earthworks, or prehistoric fields overlain by ridge-and-furrow. He follows this with a complex relationship where Roman kilns were excavated on a site later occupied by a medieval village, in turn disturbed by gravel workings that created mounds containing re-deposited Roman material. Having established the complexity of the task, Taylor moves to questions commonly asked by beginners.

One of these questions is 'how do you know that this site is a deserted medieval village and that site is just recent quarrying?'[2] Taylor's answer is that it is down to years of practical fieldwork and being widely read. Taylor also warns against the desire to demand, having found a new site: 'Well, what is it?' to which Taylor responds with more bad news, that 'there is an unfortunate tendency for beginners to develop all kinds of fanciful ideas which usually have no relationship to the truth', and a 'usually quite unnecessary tendency to make a site more important than it really is'.

It is not that I disagree with this advice. In any activity, geology and ornithology for example, experience counts for a great deal, and the inexperienced often make unrealistic claims, but it doesn't prevent people trying. At this point a common repost I have heard is that no-one would let an amateur brain surgeon loose on patients. However the dangers presented by a local historian trying to make sense of the landscape he or she is trying to understand is neither life-threatening nor cataclysmic. Undoubtedly there are difficulties in determining whether remains are earlier or later than ridge-and-furrow, but only when the remains are found in conjunction with ridge-and-furrow. People often make unrealistic claims about what they find, but as I argued in my 1984 article 'History on the Ground', as explained in Chapter One, there is a need for a helpful environment where the beginner can get some meaningful advice.

So many books on archa
eology fieldwork make interpretation sound impossible unless you have spent a lifetime doing it, and few other disciplines create such impossible barriers between the layman and the professional. There is a lot of mumbo jumbo in archaeology. Taylor's advice to the beginner, so as not to 'discourage the potential fieldworker', is that 'he concentrates on the recording, surveying and simple interpretation of details and relationships'.[3] That's probably all the local historian needs to do, but perhaps the experience to do it well is not such an insurmountable barrier. A friendlier than usual approach is to be found in Anthony Brown's *Fieldwork for Archaeologists and Local Historians* published in 1987. His Chapter Four is on the interpretation of earthworks, and provides twenty-two pages of well-illustrated guidance, which is more informative than intimidating, but while highlighting innumerable difficulties, does not explain very much about the process of interpreting evidence.

How to interpret remains of the past

There are however fairly simple steps that local historians can take to avoid the most obvious pitfalls. Indeed, one way to present knowledge acquired through fieldwork is to demonstrate firstly that you understand the difficulties in interpreting the site in question. Secondly, in reaching a personal opinion about what is there, you demonstrate the steps you have gone through to reach that decision. If someone disagrees, whether that's a letter to the editor of the local paper about what they have read in your book or article, or a criticism by a professional archaeologist, they ought to address the difficulties you encountered if they think differently. If remains are examined with some of the following questions in mind then the local historian will have given fair and balanced attention to the task.

1   Form – describing the components of the remains seen
2   How these components fit together
3   Sequence – where one component is earlier than another
4   Composition - how they are constructed and any compositional differences
5   Seeing more than what's there
6   Wear and tear – how the remains might have changed over time
7   How they relate to the immediate topography
8   The context of the remains in the wider landscape

Before embarking on a more detailed exploration of these questions, let's get one thing straight: you don't have to do all this. These ideas are optional. They are there to show you where potential pitfalls can arise, and where you can improve your interpretation technique. If there is no pressure on you to accurately understand what you are looking at, and you just want to add some fieldwork to your history explorations, you can do fairly well just forming your own opinions of what you see.

I also suspect that many people, on reading the following details, will wonder where anyone finds the time to go to such absurd lengths, or will feel that this is taking away all the fun from what, probably for many people, is just the added interest of local history fieldwork. For some readers perfectionism or thoroughness will compel them to read on; others may just switch off. So if you feel this is too much for the moment, jump to the next chapter and return to this another time, if you feel it would help.

1. Form

The first step is to identify the different forms present, or the component features. In the simplest terms you may be looking at 'mounds' or 'hollows'. Whether mounds (positive relief) or hollows (negative relief) these may be localised (such as a round or oblong mound or hollow), or a linear mound or hollow (such as a boundary bank or ditch). Sometimes all that can be said is that the ground in question is 'hummocky', 'stony' or a random scatter of low mounds and shallow depressions. Even features that are immediately recognisable can also be described in terms of their components: a trackway may be sunken or raised and may have ditches and/or banks either side. There is a very sound reason for doing this, because some components may have been re-used or adapted. A trackway may follow an older boundary bank or ditch, using the boundary to define one side of the track, while constructing a new bank and/or ditch on its other side. What appears to be a continuous bank may be made up of connected lengths of older banks, the original continuations of which have been flattened or destroyed. In addition it is important to observe whether these basic features are rounded or flat-topped or concave or flat-floored, and whether there are any specific shapes in plan or profile.

Also, look closely at the edges of common shapes. For example there might be a uniform depression (ditch) on one side, but a step down to a lower surface (a berm) and then a depression on the other. In most cases the evidence will prove quite simple and straight forward to identify, but this initial cautionary approach raises questions that need to be considered when formulating a decision about what the remains represent. It is also important, at this stage, not to anticipate ready explanations, as wishful thinking can lead the observer to overlook important clues.

2. How components fit together

The second step is to look carefully at the relationships between any close together, converging or touching components. Are they entirely separate? Do they overlap? At what angle do they meet, or would meet if the alignment projected further? Do features overlie or underlie each other? This anticipates the next question

– sequence – but at this stage simply observe the patterns on the ground. One of the dangers here is being too quick to spot 'obvious' explanations, and it is not the unwary beginner that is most likely to get caught out, but the seasoned 'expert'. Most remains are straightforward and utilitarian, and were not set out to puzzle future landscape interpreters. However where the same locations have been re-used in different ways over time, spotting the non-conforming clues is crucial, and these can be very subtle changes.

For example where two linear features meet at right angles, do they meet as if they were constructed to do so, or does one bank stop up against or just short of the other? Or has one been reduced in height and the other carried over the top of it, in which case are there any traces of the reduced bank having continued beyond its neighbour on the other side? If there are two oblong platforms next to each other, is the relationship exactly symmetrical or are they orientated slightly differently, or offset one to the other? We tend to make broad generalisations at first glance, and even see what the brain expects rather than what is actually there. With more care and attention to detail we may see unexpected deviations in patterns and shapes that we think at first ought to conform to expectations.

3. Sequence

This is where the unfortunate term 'stratigraphy' arises. Archaeology borrowed it from geology to denote the sequence of one layer above another in an excavation, and then extended the term to other contexts where there is assumed to be sequence. The basic issue here is whether one element of the site was formed before another element. These need not be in contact with one another, but they might overlap. Many sites, to all intents and purposes, only represent one event, and 'stratigraphy' is largely a scare story.

Archaeological literature makes much of ridge-and-furrow, the corrugated effect seen in fields that denotes the survival of medieval cultivation strips. These strips make up a unit of about a quarter of an acre depending on length and width, the width varying between five and ten metres mostly, but with some ridges, usually of more recent date, as narrow as 3 metres. The assumption is that ridge-and-furrow can be dated, and if remains survive in an area of ridge-and-furrow they are more likely to be later and therefore post-medieval. However this is not an exact science. It is often assumed that ridge-and-furrow ceased after parishes were reorganised into modern rectangular fields, mostly in the eighteenth century, but locally the practice continued, and some apparent ridges were constructed for drainage, such as in orchards. Conversely, some ridge-and-furrow reverted to pasture long before enclosure made this system redundant, so something overlying could be late medieval rather than indisputably post-medieval.

Nor does ridge-and-furrow preclude the existence of earlier earthworks. Sometimes the ridges can be seen to override earlier earthworks, or a pre-existing enclosure is adapted for cultivation after it has ceased to serve its original function, by having cultivation ridges developed within it or partly overlapping it. This happens with disused fish ponds, for example, because the soil in the floor of the former pond is rich in nutrients. Some enclosure banks, even if obsolete, were

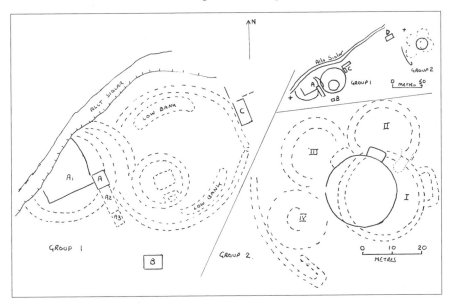

17 Douchary sheepfolds, Wester Ross. These circular sheepfolds are built overlapping the foundations of their predecessors – it's all about 'stratigraphy'.

respected, perhaps because they could be used again. The important point to make about stratigraphy is that it is a difficult and uncertain science, and as difficult for experts as beginners. If the local historian is wary, and makes appropriate observations, such as those concerned with how components fit together (2 above), that is probably sufficient.

It is worth some diversion here about 'stratigraphy' such where one enclosure overlies another. Taylor describes a typical problem, a circular sheepfold overlying two earlier huts, on Tinkler Crags, on Askerton North Moor in Cumberland.[4] While the sequence here is obvious, the underlying enclosures need not be significantly older than the overlying one. Circular sheepfolds were often rebuilt to one side but overlapping a ruinous predecessor, so as to lay fresh foundations, while having a ready supply of stone from the previous fold to undertake a careful rebuild. Equally a sheepfold could be built on a site where there are remains of much older enclosures, where overlapping the older foundations adds stability, and again provides ready materials. However if huts were needed as shelters where shepherds could camp by the fold overnight, these might be constructed later than the sheepfold with one side sharing the outside of the sheepfold wall for stability. Both round and rectangular sheepfolds have externally built huts against the walls, in the same fashion as Taylor witnessed at Tinkler Crags, which could actually have been closely contemporary with the sheepfold. 'Stratigraphy' only implies sequence, and the veracity of sequence needs to be carefully checked, but is no guarantee, and it tells us nothing about the passage of time.

An example of this is the sheep gathering station known as The Douchary, in a very remote valley 12 kilometres south-east of Ullapool, Wester Ross, in northern Scotland. Documentation as far back as 1589, when the pasture and shielings of Dowchorrie were protected in settlement of a land dispute, show that The Douchary was an important asset up until the early twentieth century. The most recent remains here are large circular and rectangular sheep enclosures (Plate 16), and several standing rectangular buildings. However there are remains of older circular sheepfolds which clearly overlie the foundations of many predecessors (Figure 17) and in one case the present circle overlaps four precursors, each in turn overlapping the one before.[5] If a sheepfold lasts say 75 years of repairs before being built again, and the last of these was built in 1900, the first might have been built in 1600. Yet in so many instances, overlapped foundations are assumed to be ancient, and at Durness, 20 miles north of Ullapool, in almost every case where a sheepfold overlies an earlier circular enclosure, the latter has been identified as prehistoric. One argument I have heard to support this is that medieval and post-medieval Scots didn't know how to construct circular enclosures, so the overlapped foundation must be thousands of years older. The safest policy for the local historian is to look out for sequence evidence, and describe any apparent sequencing when writing about a site, and perhaps attempt either documentary research or test out folk memory to find out whether the sequences are recent or ancient. There may be a retired farmer or farm labourer in your locality who can tell you how things used to be done.

4. Composition

It is very important to look for changes in the way features are constructed. Thus, even if the superficial configuration looks consistent, a change in construction might indicate a different phase, or merely a repair. This includes such compositional materials as earth and stone mixed, small stones, large stones, stone wall footings with rubble in between, or twin drystone walls with a gap between. If it is necessary to disturb the ground such as lifting turf with a trowel, seek permission from the landowner first, and do not do so on sites which are scheduled or likely to be sensitive (which includes not only heritage sites but those with ecological importance). Normally it should be sufficient to observe, from close examination, whether a mound has earthen or stony composition, and whether this changes in different parts of the mound.

There is a very puzzling enclosure within the hillfort known as Burnswark, near Ecclefechan (Dumfries and Galloway, Scotland). Plates 17 and 18 show Burnswark from afar and close up. It has long been described as 'heart-shaped' (Figure 18), and is currently explained as a seventeenth-century artillery fort. However there are many variations in the composition of its walls, and it probably has a long and very complex history. As Burnswark was common grazing up to the nineteenth century, one potential culprit for all these different elements are shepherds and herdsmen filling time by enhancing the enclosure as somewhere to shelter, while taking advantage of the view afforded across the hill pastures. The writer's ancestor John Murray farmed just south of Burnswark, and used the summit as common, and might have known the explanation. The curve of the wall on the south-west side is very different from that on the north-west, while on the involuted top of the heart on the south-east side there are at least four different compositions. It

1 The River Ribble, east of Preston, is diverted southwards by the cliffs of Red Scar, rising above the trees on the left of this picture, while the confluence of Tun Brook is under trees in the distance.

2 The footbridge on Ribble Way crossing Tun Brook; a glimpse of the narrow confines.

3 The fallen tree on the site of Lee Castle, in the roots of which the author found more than 300 sherds of medieval pottery, mainly thirteenth–fourteenth century. The tree, which the author had climbed on as a child, blew over in a gale in December 1984. In suburbia, history on the ground can be that close.

4 An Dunan, Kylesku, Sutherland, showing the rising steps within the wall structure that had been dug out by a holidaymaker several years before.

5 Clachtoll Broch, Sutherland, inside one of the guard chambers (the red and white scale is 1 metre long).

6 Map showing Vitower, Ower and Goathorn on south side of Poole Harbour, Dorset. *Reproduced by permission of Ordnance Survey on behalf of HMSO © Crown copyright (2008) All rights reserved. Ordnance Survey Licence Number 100048555.*

7 Titchfield Abbey, Hampshire. An early inspiration to the author to combine documentary research with fieldwork.

8 Titchfield Abbey excavations, part of a stone-lintelled culvert.

9 Overlee Park, near Glasgow, where the author found platforms, one of which turned out to be a mine shaft. The park is in the foreground; the woodland lies on the east bank of the White Cart Water.

10 A view of Dunkeld rooftops towards Dunkeld Cathedral ruins, with a tree-covered Bishop's Hill rising beyond it; the probable site of Bishop's Castle.

11 The north side of Dunkeld Cathedral and the west end of the medieval town, where there were once a number of prebendal manses and other buildings.

12 West Revoch Cairn, Eaglesham, near Glasgow. These ruinous remains survive, where others had been entirely removed, because in the nineteenth century it was confused with another cairn nearby.

13 The Roundabout, Rapley, near Bagshot. This woodland shot shows the actual location of a Roman settlement described in 1783; boundary changes displaced the Rapley placename northwards.

14 Rapley Lake. Artificial, it may cover part of a Roman settlement.

15 Site of eighteenth-century Scone including former market cross, near Perth.

16 Douchary, in Rhidorroch Forest, Wester Ross, one of the extant round sheepfolds where successive enclosures overlap: a good example of 'stratigraphy'.

17 Burnswark, Dumfriesshire. Within the Iron Age fort, on its summit, is a mysterious multi-period heart-shaped enclosure that demonstrates the importance of understanding composition. Burnswark is surrounded by Roman camps and practice works, and a complex of medieval and post-medieval enclosures.

18 Close-up of Burnswark from the south. The heart-shape is on the summit, and the author has plotted numerous earthworks around known enclosures at the base.

19 Kirktonmoor Cairn, Eaglesham, near Glasgow. This prehistoric burial cairn owes its survival to being greatly altered over time, through encroachment and re-use, so that it wasn't raided by treasure hunters, like so many others here.

20 Lassintullich, near Kinloch Rannoch, Perthshire, said to be the location of an early monastic settlement, but is it archaeology? The mound with the chapel and graveyard is far right of the knoll with the ledge, and the rock-cut remains are on the ridge behind above the farmhouse. *Photograph by C.M.Welsh.*

21 Another view of Lassintullich, from the south.

22 Trees on the march, Ridorroch, near Ullapool. Progressive creep on this hillside has displaced the tree roots so that they appear to be marching downhill.

23 Fire-exposed road section on Houndkirk Moor. The pale ashen surface results from the sandstone metalling and can be compared to the darker burnt peat either side.

24 Where the road crosses Burbage Brook. The remains of the bridge are in the middle distance, and the road climbs the farther bank as a long incline rising to the left.

25 Winyard's Nick, near Hathersage. This photograph shows different levels of passage through the nick as it was worn deeper over the centuries by successive use. The author's road passes through at the highest level on the right, giving credence to its apparent antiquity.

26 On Bakeham Hill, Surrey. This 1982 photograph shows the location where Roman remains were found in 1835 near the original site of Bakeham House.

27 Devil's Highway embankment east of Virginia Water; a swath of ridges and scarps marks the course of the old London Road, but includes a linear bank consistent with other evidence of the earthwork known as the Devil's Highway. In the photograph the red and white ranging pole is only 1 metre long.

28 Busby Glen promontory fort, found by the author in 1972, on realising that the curved alignment of four massive stones was part of the foundations of the fort rampart.

29 Bruce Motte, Lochmaben. The photograph is taken from Gallowshill where the author found an annexe, possibly dating from the time of Edward I's Scottish campaigns. It is surprising that the rival summit at Gallowshill was not previously investigated.

30 Roxburgh Castle, on the right of the photo, looking up the River Teviot.

31 Roxborough Castle across the River Tweed. There are remains west and south-west of the castle hill.

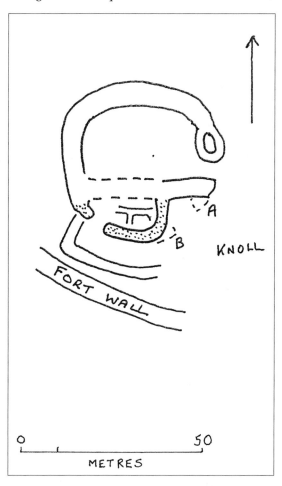

18 Burnswark Hill, Dumfriesshire – the heart-shaped enclosure which contains so many compositional elements.

was excavated in 1966 by George Jobey, who found part of the circuit had at first been built of turf and stone, which after collapse had been rebuilt and revetted with inner and outer drystone facings.[6] Romano-British material was found in the original wall remains. On the involuted side of the 'heart shape' (between A and B on Figure 18) the curves and the sides of the V represent four different construction styles, and there are foundations corresponding to the northern side of the V carried across the interior (broken lines). There are also foundations of an annexe on the south side (stippled on Figure 18) and foundations underlying the involuted walls (A and B). A more likely explanation is that the enclosure was originally circular, then reduced to a D-shape, which had an enclosure annexed to it, before finally being modified, a little artistically, as a heart shape.

Given the emphasis on 'stratigraphy' in archaeological literature, composition seems to get little mention, perhaps because it can best be investigated by excavation. However few sites get excavated. The local historian should look out for compositional and constructional changes because, though they sometimes represent different styles or phases of construction of a single feature, they are

19 Abington Park, Northampton – ghost enclosure. Against a very complex backdrop of former houses and associated garden plots there appears to be a circular enclosure here, with an oval annexe to the south east.

also a warning to look out for both 'stratigraphy' and the coincidence of several different features. It is important to check whether the differently fashioned elements belong to different features, of which traces may be continued beyond the area of immediately obvious remains.

5. Seeing more than what is there

This is a cautionary tale –there was a time when wallpaper, carpets and curtains were richly patterned. Those patterns always seemed to reveal hidden shapes like a cowled monk, or a gnarled face, or a stooped figure, or a dog or something else that, if you looked hard enough, or long enough, magically emerged from that pattern. But if you asked another family member, or a visitor, if they could see the same thing, they either couldn't, or tactfully weren't so sure, or saw something completely different that you in turn could not see. The trouble with the pattern of remains on the ground is that you do, very easily, see shapes and outlines that may not actually be there in reality, and even if these hidden patterns are realistic, it may only be possible to prove them by excavation.

A personal insight into this experience is at Abington Park in Northampton (which crops up again in Chapter Eight). Figure 19 shows the layout of tofts or individual property units on one side of a street in a deserted medieval village. Here there is a regular pattern of house platforms next to the hollow way that forms the street, with regular boundaries dividing each house, and a plot of land behind each house, from its neighbours, and each plot has an end wall. To the writer there appears to be a circular feature lying across the width of two garden plots (Figure 19). This is much more problematic because, although I can see curved elements, the circle has some straight facets, which have become components of not quite linear plot divides, and some linear features in the plot layout look like elements of the circle. The writer has examined this feature many times, trying to decide if it really exists. Without excavation it would be difficult to convince others just on the basis of speculation. However what appears to be there is a circular enclosure, about 15 metres internal diameter, formed by a bank about 10 metres thick.

The way to get round this uncertainty though is to explore a number of possible interpretations. This takes a certain amount of self-discipline and honesty. You need to identify three or four genuine possibilities, and follow them through in detail, weighing up the evidence in favour and the evidence against. In the case of the Abington Park earthwork, the plot strips are the dominant feature. The circular enclosure might just be a composite of unrelated elements resulting from garden digging, or industrial activity, or additional buildings on the plot. It might represent something simpler, such as a pond or the containment of an industrial structure, superseded and overlain when one large plot was divided into two. By exploring several interpretations in a balanced way, the local historian can offer a considered argument that the perceived enclosure may have existed, but other explanations should be considered. That is about as much as anyone can do in the absence of resources to carry out an excavation.

6. Wear and tear

Natural processes alter the profile and shape of remains over time. The culprits include heavy rain and consequent surface flow washing away the soil and undermining stone structures, and freezing and thawing in winter dislodging stones. Plant roots, especially trees, can change the configuration of the surface and buried layers by lifting and displacing them, and if toppled can wrench up part of the structure, or leave behind small mounds or hollows when the roots decay. Animal burrows can tunnel through remains and displace the excavated material to the burrow mouth, and collapsed burrows also change the surface topography. Human activity also erodes, by cutting into mounds in the process of new constructions, and by levelling and cultivation. It is not unheard of for farmers, displeased at the nuisance of having a protected antiquity on their land, to shave a little closer with the plough each year, or do a bit of subtle relocation of stones, and diminish the size of the unwelcome intruder from the past. This is one of the reasons why I think local historians should be encouraged to monitor change to monuments in their area.

In Chapter One, I gave several examples of the value of monitoring for change due to human agents, such as the unofficial excavation of a dun in Sutherland, and the burying of a Lanarkshire motte in a tip. As indicated above, the agent in wear and tear can be human as well. Recalling West Revoch Cairn in Chapter 3, there is another cairn near Eaglesham, at North Kirktonmoor (Plate 19). Again it is first recorded in a farm plan in 1789, but suffered many and varied alterations over time, ending up as a trapezoidal mound 22 metres by 15, with a rough building constructed on top. The encroachments had been made by cultivation, with the removed stone being piled on the original, but close inspection showed the original outline survived.[7]

It is important to look at any grouping of remains to see if they have been reduced in size by cultivation or landscaping. For example, if there are ploughed fields in proximity, is the current edge of a group of features likely to be its true extent, or has some of it been removed by ploughing? If the line of an old boundary wall or fence crosses the remains are the remains any less clear on one side compared to the other? Has there been erosion by a nearby stream in flood? Has there been quarrying, either of underlying natural resources or material removed in relation to the observed features? Has material been added to the site, such as rubbish or stones cleared from adjacent fields, and could this have concealed evidence? All these clues are important, as remains that now appear roughly circular may once have been rectangular, and conversely an irregular sided feature may once have been circular. The remains may represent just one small part of a larger feature, most of which has been destroyed by ploughing, in which case air photographs (Chapter Five) may be useful to see if any crop or soil marks reveal the lost extent.

7. Topography

The seventh step is to look at the remains in relation to the natural topography. Are they on level or sloping ground? If remains extend in one direction, either the long axis of a group of features or a linear mound or hollow, are they aligned across a contour, or parallel to the contour or at an angle to the contour? Does that relationship change anywhere? Are there any variations in level within the group of features, such as natural or artificial terracing, natural gullies or hollow ways traversing the site?

An obvious example arises with water power. If the remains suggest the site of a mill, there needs to be a means of conveying water along the valley side from a point at which water can be captured at a dam or a weir. This conveyance needs to provide sufficient head of water to turn a water wheel, although with older mill sites with either a horizontal wheel or an undershot wheel that might be less than a metre; for more recent mills the water needs to have been raised two or three metres above the level of the stream nearest the remains being investigated. This may even mean a small pond being formed at that elevation, to store the captured water. If the remains include a terrace or a bank along the hillside that might indicate how the water was carried to the mill, this ought to show a gradual incline from the source to the suspected mill to ensure a steady flow of water. If there is insufficient evidence that this is feasible, it doesn't preclude the remains of the water supply having been destroyed by cultivation or landscaping in the intervening time, but it does prompt a reassessment of the remains suspected of being a mill, in case another explanation might be forthcoming.

Another application of topography arises when looking at defences. If a site has natural advantages such as steep slopes, or even a near-vertical drop, the defences are likely to make use of this. But even on less steep sites a steepening of the natural gradient is a good location to construct ramparts and ditches, because part of the elevation comes from the natural slope, and less elevation has to be created from the artificial constructs. If linear features enclose a possible defended area, if they cross the contour obliquely, rather than follow the contour, and there is no obvious advantage in doing so, or the advantage of steeper parts of the slope are missed, then a defensive origin is less likely.

An example is the large undated 'hillfort' at Borough Hill, Daventry, in Northamptonshire. A plan published in 1823 by the historian John Baker, while

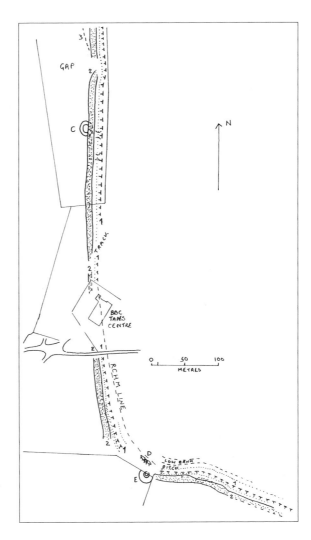

20 Borough Hill, Daventry. The official circuit leaves the natural scarp here to cross level ground at the south-west corner of the fort, even though remains of the defences can still be seen following the scarp.

exaggerating the dimensions of the fort, shows the plan much as it appears today in one by the Royal Commission. However the circuit in the south-west corner of the fort has been destroyed by ploughing since Baker's time, and the course of the defences here are based on a drawing by Edgar in 1923.[8] Whereas Baker shows the defences bulging outwards at the south-west angle, to take advantage of a projecting shoulder of the hilltop, Edgar cuts the corner, linking the ends of the surviving remains of the defences on the west and south (Figure 20). For a fort that round its entire circuit makes good use of the crest of the slope around the summit, this sudden decision to strike inwards from the natural crest and cross flatter ground over the south-west shoulder seems very strange, but as the fort defences have been ploughed out here, Edgar's route is taken for granted.

The situation is confused by localised quarrying at the end of the extant defences, making the ditch appear larger, and cutting into the crest of the slope. Edgar's course of the defences follows the receding scarp produced by quarrying, and veers south-south-east of this across flatter ground, where it looses the advantage of the available change in elevation. In fact faint traces of the defences can still be seen on the natural scarp as shown by Baker in 1823. It pays to take topography into account.

8. Wider context

For this we go back to the criteria explored in Chapter Two. If we are to avoid Taylor's concern about beginners making a site more important than it is, and having fanciful notions as to its origins, we need to look at feasibility. The questions suggested in Chapter Two were to look at how a site fits into the landscape, and any constraints in this relationship, communications, water supply, security and defence, if these apply. It is good advice to look for commonplace or simple explanations first, and consider any greater significance with more caution over the criteria examined. If looking at remains as those of some sort of fortification – whether an Iron Age fort or a castle – there should not be better suited sites in proximity. Look at how other defensive installations tackle choice of site in the country roundabout, and what form they take.

It is a good idea to produce a sketchplan, in order to check whether the observed features still make sense when formalised on paper. Many of the illustrations in this book are simple sketchplans at the time of fieldwork, and sometimes used to illustrate interim reports, but were never intended for publication. The fact that they are published now serves to illustrate the value of first impressions rather than the intimidating formality encountered in many archaeology books. Many archaeology books recommend formal survey at this stage, whether plane-tabling, theodolite traverses, or global positioning systems, but that means setting out ranging rods at key points across the site even if you are not yet certain of whether these are significant, and plans produced by surveying too early can miss important details. Far better to produce a simple transect with offsets, either measured with a tape or even paced, merely to get sufficient understanding of the relative position of features. Be prepared, if opportunities allow, to revisit several times to modify and add detail to the sketchplan. If you are then confident of what you wish to record, there are a number of textbooks, including archaeology textbooks, to recommend the best way to make an accurate record, ranging from Taylor to Bowden.[9]

The detailed questions above may appear rather laborious, especially if the evidence looks obvious and easy to interpret, and it must be a matter for personal judgement, how far you choose to go with such evaluation. However local historians who will happily spend all day in a record office questing for a single documentary clue, might equally be prepared to spends at least several hours, if not a whole day, trying to unravel complex evidence on the ground. For the local historian hoping to write about their interpretation of the historic landscape, or give talks to their local society, the safest strategy is to take a bit of care over interpretation, and try to avoid missing anything obvious, as others writing in the future may not be merciful in pointing out the disagreement or error.

Chapter Five

MAPS AND AIR PHOTOGRAPHS

It might seem odd to approach maps as a separate chapter from one dealing with documents, but I wanted to approach this a different way, and show how aerial photographs can help to make sense of them. In a book trying to give a visual perspective of local history through the evidence on the ground, other visual forms, such as maps and air photographs, play a very important part. Of course a lot can be done by walking and looking, but as a way of recovering a sense of the past vertical air photographs are an asset. They do not show everything, either because of obscuring vegetation, or lack of meaningful contrast, but they do allow a broader perspective or synoptic view of the landscape. They also show many features that may not be obvious on a map.

Vertical air photos

In this chapter I have placed the emphasis on vertical air photographs, which is the view directly downwards from beneath an aircraft, whereas the reader may well come across oblique photographs. These are views taken from the side of an aircraft, through a window or hatch, looking across the landscape at an angle. This angle may be one looking steeply down on the ground below, or at a shallower angle towards the horizon. Archaeology uses oblique aerial photographs to detect surface manifestations of the remains of the past: crop marks, soil marks, low relief revealed by light and shadow. This could be a useful tool for the local historian, as assuredly the study area will include discoveries made by air photo archaeology. The classic text *Air Photo Interpretation for Archaeologists* by D.R. Wilson was originally published by Batsford in 1982, but is now available in a new edition by Tempus released in 2000. Unless local historians have access to flights and suitable cameras they will have to rely on other people's oblique air photos, and these are really snaps of what caught one person's eye from the right angle, in the right conditions on the right day. They probably didn't look so good from other directions, and sometimes the features captured in these photographs didn't show up so well on other flights. While vertical air photographs can be used to detect archaeology, their main benefit to the local historian is to look at the pattern of natural features (such as water courses), field boundaries and traces of former boundaries and features that might help to interpret old maps and plans.

The most likely place to find suitable vertical air photographs is in a county or other central library, although occasionally these may be held by a planning department, where they are less readily accessible to the public, or in a university or college. In the 1970s and 1980s many local authorities were persuaded, for planning purposes, to invest in air photo coverage. This usually consists of a series of parallel flights across the county, with some overlap between flights, and often 60% overlap between photographs along the flightline to enable photos to be viewed in stereo, otherwise with 30% overlap. Sometimes these are in colour, but often just black and white; colour may look good, but if there is a subtle range of different grey shades on the monochrome photograph the latter can be just as informative. Another option is to purchase the air photo coverage, either from a national centre or from the main commercial organisations. Older photographs are sometimes also available, including wartime or early post-war photographs, but the ground cover may be patchy, and the quality, in terms of a clear picture and range of grey scale, may be poorer. There is likely to be a mixture of vertical and oblique air photographs. The value of these older photographs is they show the landscape before modern ploughing and urban expansion removed so much of the evidence of the past. A third source is through websites, such as Google and GetMapping, which provide a mixture of satellite imagery and vertical air photographs; there are also atlases and photo-based street maps. At the time of writing larger scale imagery, suitable for historical work, occurs mainly around towns and in the more populous rural areas, with many areas only providing small-scale and coarse resolution imagery that affords little detail, but this is progressively improving. With a bit of searching and negotiation local historians should be able to access some sort of air photo cover to examine. Your local Historic Environment Record (HER) will hold oblique archaeology photos, and there are national depositories as well, such as English Heritage. There are also resources available online.

Depending on the scale used, mostly between 1:5,000 and 1:20,000 scale (approximately 12 inches to 3 inches to the mile; 50 to 200 metres to a centimetre), a single photo about 20 centimetres square will cover between 100 metres square and 400 metres square approximately (most sets of individual air photos are around 1:10,000). The smaller scales, such as are available on websites, can only be used for general reference, but even at 1:10,000 scale the archaeological detail is limited, a structure 50 metres in diameter being only 5 millimetres across. At 1:100,000 scale the same feature is therefore only 0.5 millimetres across. There are now many small-scale paper air photo atlases and maps. *The Photographic Atlas of England*, published in 2001, mainly relies on 1:72,000 scale for rural areas and 1:4500 scale for urban areas. In these rural maps one centimetre square on the image is 720 metres square on the ground, which is too coarse for local history, although a useful resource for understanding the layout and character of landscapes. Photomap street maps provide areas of landscape around the fringes of towns at 1:100 scale or better, which are useful for town-based fieldwork where the overlay of streets and street names permits. With improved resolution satellite imagery is also a viable option for looking at large areas, with the constraint that, if resolution is 10 metres, the smallest thing on the image is a dot, depending on scale, with perhaps less than a millimetre representing 10 metres square on the ground. At that scale and resolution you cannot see cars or dustbins, and family-sized houses will not be well defined, however you can determine a lot about the spatial arrangement of fields, routeways and watercourses.

Modern maps

Modern maps are useful aids to local history because they provide a ready guide to spatial relationships in the landscape, such as where roads lead to and how features fit into the landscape. They can be used to explore and to resolve problems in the same way as discussed for fieldwork in Chapter Two. The ideal scales to work at are Ordnance Survey 1:25,000 scale (2.5 inch to the mile) and 1:10,000 scale (approximately 6 inches to the mile). With the former the current Explorer series covers around 30 kilometres square, whereas the previous Pathfinder series covered just two ten-kilometre squares side by side. These are sufficient to see most field boundaries and watercourses, but roads are shown between 0.5 and 1 millimetre wide, representing between 12 and 25 metres on the ground, which is an exaggeration of reality that can quickly diminish accuracy when there are lots of roads. Names on a map may be between one and two millimetres high, with six to nine letters per centimetre, partly concealing a block of land perhaps 50 by 250 metres, so maps at 1:25,000 scale are very cluttered with information, and compromises have to be made. The alternative is to work with 1:10,000 scale maps, which may have to be ordered through larger bookshops but can be accessed in public libraries. Here the area covered is usually only 5 kilometres square, but the details are close to accurate, with roads shown a little above true width. At this scale it is easier to detect slight changes in field boundaries and the courses of streams. In addition many public libraries will have maps at 1:2,500 scale (25 inches to the mile) which are essential when looking at urban areas, and for tracing the fine detail of watercourses. Going in the opposite direction of scale, however, is counter-productive. At 1:50,000 scale Landranger maps and their predecessors at 1:63,000 (one inch to the mile) are too small for local history use, as no field boundaries are shown and much of the essential detail is overly simplified (roads on 1:50,000 scale maps are shown around 50 metres wide).

Old maps and plans

The next part of the equation covers maps and plans produced in the past. There are five main groups of old maps and plans:

- larger scale county maps from the mid-eighteenth century
- early Ordnance Survey editions back to mid to late nineteenth century
- estate maps ranging from all or part of a parish down to individual property units
- enclosure award maps
- tithe award maps

While the improved maps in the eighteenth century at scales of one or two inches to the mile are mostly at county level, there were exceptions, including a detailed survey of Scotland by William Roy between 1747 and 1755, created as a means of suppressing rebellion after the Jacobite rising of 1745. Amongst the older Ordnance Survey maps 1:2,500 scale maps are perhaps the most useful for the amount of historical detail, otherwise 1:10,560 (6 inch to the mile) scale maps are sufficient. In the late eighteenth and early nineteenth century there were usually county maps available with comparable detail if less precision. Estate maps were usually created to record land improvements and to facilitate day-to-day management, or to promote the sale of a property, or just to impress the guests at country houses. Sometimes both estate maps and maps accompanying terriers or lists of land holdings show the pre-enclosure division into furlongs, and even the individual strips, numbered according to ownership or the yearly division of lots. This category can also be extended to include property maps, down to individual house plots, drawn up for sale or mortgage, which often accompany written deeds, and are sometimes drawn in the margins of deeds, showing components of a property such as house, outbuildings, yard and well, and the owners of the adjacent properties.

Enclosure award maps were drawn to support the Enclosure Acts and show the resulting allocation of land. Tithe award maps were drawn up in the 1840s in order to quantify the landholdings, wealth and ability of parishioners to pay a portion of their income to the upkeep of the church and the clergy. However these are useful sources of field names, and help to understand land ownership.

Old maps at region, county or district level cover a range of cartographic resources from the earliest representations up to present-day Ordnance Survey maps, but for the purposes of local history useful sources first appear in the eighteenth century, when techniques for ensuring spatial accuracy, such as triangulation, were introduced. Earlier exceptions include the vignettes on some late sixteenth- to early seventeenth-century county maps showing town plans, or simulated bird's eye views of towns. The sorts of things that these provide that could help local history on the ground are the courses of obsolete roads, the sites of buildings, including functional buildings such as mills, manor houses or farmsteads, and depictions of antiquities, usually recorded as landmarks.

Usually a more focused, localised source, old plans range from estate or enclosure awards at parish level down to the boundaries and configuration of individual property units. Again these are usually from the eighteenth century onwards, but can be much earlier. They generally show different kinds of information from modern large-scale Ordnance Survey plans (1:10,000 or 6 inch to the mile; 1:2,500 or 25 inch to the mile and larger). Modern plans show legally important details (cadastral) such as property boundaries and access routes, but do not tell us who owns or utilises the land, or what the land is used for (beyond symbols and shading for certain categories). Their eighteenth- and nineteenth-century counterparts also show legal boundaries, but often show owners and tenants, (and accompanying documents may contain owner and tenant histories), as well as information about land-use, either on the map or by means of letters or numbers keyed to an associated document or schedule. As such they are often useful to local historians.

Combining resources

Used together, air photographs, modern maps and older maps and plans provide a fertile resource for the local historian. While modern maps show current boundaries and buildings, air photographs show the patterns and textures within this framework, providing extra detail and sometimes detecting traces of the past. These in turn help to understand the information on older maps and plans, showing where change has taken place, and helping to locate the recorded past within the accurately mapped present. There is a fourth arm to this relationship, checking the evidence on the ground. However it is not always feasible to reach all the places seen on an old plan, and it is not easy to determine subtleties in the direction of tracks and boundaries without the advantage of modern maps and air photographs to build up a picture. Everything previously discussed about fieldwork can be explored in an armchair or by spreading out on a desktop a combination of air photos, modern and early maps, but at some point the resulting revelations and curiosities need to be explored on the ground.

One notable distinction from archaeology is that these resources seem seldom to be interplayed. Whether using vertical or oblique air photographs, the patterns of elevated features or crop marks recorded seem seldom to be checked on the ground, the argument being that the air photographs supersede the need for fieldwork, and ground checking can be carried out when the need arises for detailed fieldwork or excavation. Moreover air photo archaeology discoveries seem seldom to be checked for more modern explanation, such as may be found on old maps and plans; nor are they checked for possible natural origins, as discussed in Chapter Six. As previously observed, the motivations of archaeologist and local historian differ, the one concerned with the discovery and classification of individual finds, whereas the local historian may be content to be able to describe the landscape and explain the context, even where actual remains of the past are elusive.

Most local historians are unlikely to embark upon their own air photo archaeology, though they might take advantage of the opportunity to go up in a plane or a helicopter or a balloon, to see the landscape from above. Archaeological air photo collections that others have produced may help to build up a picture of an area's past, but only the past someone else spotted, when conditions were just right. The local historian is likely to want to explore how such evidence fits into the landscape, and have recourse to maps and photographs to supplement fieldwork. The interpretation of oblique air photographs can be quite difficult to integrate, because they are so specific, and have perspectives that are not readily related to the map. The reason that the vertical air photographs best suit the local historian is that they help show spatial relationships over large areas, which assist in both fieldwork and in researching the evidence on old maps and plans.

Used in conjunction with modern large-scale Ordnance Survey maps vertical air photos make a difference, both in colouring the information from the maps, and in turn helping to make sense of information on old maps and plans, which may be inaccurate in terms of consistent scale and spatial relationships over an extensive landscape. Also, for landscapes that are now built over, wartime or 1960s, 70s or 80s air photographs can help interpret that past that cannot be readily related to the present. Using vertical air photographs together with modern maps, it is easy, with practice, to go exploring around this static pictorial landscape. Whereas walking it would take days to cover the same ground as thoroughly, and there are often restrictions as to where you can walk, such as private land or physical barriers, from the air you can cover the ground rapidly and with only the obscuration of trees as an obstacle, to see the relationships between features. You can explore the possibilities for past routeways or examine in plan the defensive potential of different heights or promontories. You can use the air photographs in the same way as suggested for fieldwork in Chapter Two, to pose questions and assess possible answers.

The main problem with using vertical air photographs is that you have to get used to seeing everything from its upward profile rather than from its side as you would from the ground. An area of deciduous woodland for example, which we are used to seeing as rising branching stems and a leafy canopy, looks more like a greengrocer's tray of cauliflowers and broccoli heads on an air photograph. Elephants from the air look like rather large mice, with big ears but rather short tails. Houses have to be identified from their roof characteristics. There is a classic children's game of guessing shapes seen from above, such as a Mexican riding a bicycle – a circle within a circle for the hat part and the wide brim, and two aligned strokes either side for the wheels of the bicycle. However, in other respects the air photo is much like a map, with the same plan view of field boundaries and roadways. The difference is the photographic rendering of surface characteristics, which sometimes include clues as to the course of a long removed field boundary, or the site of a house.

The literature on using old maps

The potential of estate maps was colourfully itemised by Emmison in 1966 to include, amongst forty or so possibilities, mines, grottoes, icehouses, windmills, almshouses, dovecotes and pounds.[1] This is useful information, not just on the grounds of identifying mines and windmills, but as a resource of more recent explanations for remains the fieldworker might otherwise suppose to be of greater antiquity. However the key features for the purposes of local history on the ground include defining the curtilege and internal details of a manor house, the layout of fish ponds, vernacular buildings, water mills with their means of acquiring a head of water, and suchlike. Occasionally antiquities are shown as landmarks, and further clues, either to the past or to recent land-use, may be found in field names. The pioneering guide to using old maps as a resource for local history was J.B. Harley, whose book *Maps for the Local Historian* was published in 1972.[2] He examined the practicalities and potential of town maps, estate maps, enclosure and tithe maps together with route maps, marine charts and county maps.

More recently, there has been a good synthesis of old maps by Paul Hindle (1998) which covers county maps, estate, enclosure and tithe maps, town plans, transport maps and Ordnance Survey maps.[3] Hindle's book is an important watershed in local history thinking as it addresses the need for local historians to make better use of map evidence, where previously there has been distrust and neglect. His comments on the accuracy of eighteenth-century county maps and estate maps provide an effective background to what may or may not be depicted and with what degree of reliability. He also provides important insight into the use of surveyors' drafts in the preparation of enclosure maps, as these may show the landscape before enclosure, while the finished map shows the new order. Hindle picks out three ways of using old maps: in terms of the history of cartography, for the information they contain, and thirdly, and importantly context, with regard to the reasons for making maps and the expectations of map purchasers and commissioners at different times. Sometimes the demand for maps was to visualise the lie of the land in broad terms, and for those customers various cartographers attempted to produce county and district maps over large areas of the country, with varying success in balancing outgoings and income. By the eighteenth century customers were looking for accuracy rather than art, both in terms of spatial representation though more effective triangulation, and for detail about the landscape. Pioneers included Thomas Jeffreys, John Rocque, Burdett, and John Taylor.[4]

The maps that are of most use to local historians, however, had more fundamental purposes. Some estate maps and more localised plans were produced during sale and purchase of land, or shortly after purchase to assess the resource, and needed to show boundaries, extents such as acreages of fields, any shared or common rights, and any restrictions on a property. Some maps showed the layout of improvements, such as parks, gardens and vistas. Others were specialised such as enclosure award maps which recorded the division of land under the Enclosure Acts, and tithe award maps which showed property extents and productivity as a basis for assessment of tithe payment to the parish church. The important point to make here is that the information useful to local historians depends very much on the purpose of the map and what would thus be excluded. On some maps the useful content is hidden in odd spaces and shapes.

Hindle also makes some very useful observations about survival, accuracy, generalisation and the finding of such maps. Sometimes few copies of a specialist map were made, and these may have been lost or damaged. The usefulness of a map often depends on whether features are drawn relative to one another both spatially and directionally (whether they are planimetrically accurate and referenced to reliable geodetic coordinates). If this is not the case it may prove difficult to interpret them in relation to modern maps, because boundaries are not on present alignments or intervening spaces are a different size and shape. On the other hand, in order to provide clear uncluttered information at a given scale some of the evidence is simplified or generalised, such as reducing an irregular line to the nearest equivalent straight or curve, replacing frequent objects by a symbol, or leaving out details altogether. If something was not important in the context of the intended use of the map, such as property of neighbouring landowners or features not relevant to the context in hand, they were not shown. Lastly useful maps and plans are not always readily available, some being in private collections, or held by institutions that do not normally allow access, or in storage, or undergoing conservation, but may be available as photographic copies, transcripts or on microfiche. Increasingly collections are publicly accessible on line, but the reasons for availability may be about cartographers, or design, or public interest rather than the specific needs of local historians.

Part of the information on old maps and plans that is greatly valued by historians and archaeologists alike comprises place names, field names, house and feature names. This is a vast subject field, covered by authors such as F.M. Stenton, Margaret Gelling, the English Place Name Society and John Field's study of English field names.[5] The subject matter is already familiar to most local historians, and includes such themes as clues to the course of Roman and Saxon roads, early defended settlements, distinguishing names of Danish, Saxon and Celtic origin, and tracing boundaries from Saxon charters. With reference to old maps and plans there is an essential vocabulary describing structures for land organisation at various scales, and names that inform about the topography and usability of land.

One of the issues uncovered in writing this book has been the gap between the needs of local historians and archaeologists in the way they approach fieldwork. Archaeologists tend to look at discrete evidence of the past. Local historians, while welcoming evidence of the past as subject matter, also need to know about the character of past landscapes. Much of the value of old maps and plans will be in helping to elucidate topographical conundrums in historical accounts. Unless the potential benefit of finding surviving evidence of the past from information on old maps is clearly demonstrated, it may be difficult to convince local historians of the value. Much of the writing on fieldwork for local historians has been by archaeological writers with archaeological perspectives, and their approach to air photographs, modern maps and old maps and plans has been purely about site detection. The easiest approach for local historians to take is to ask questions as they peruse the maps, just as they would do in the field, and cross-refer old map and air photo to help in this process.

The best treatment of both modern and older maps and plans by an archaeologist writing for local historians as well is Chapter Five in Brown (1987) entitled 'Maps and the Fieldworker'.[6] Brown explores the use of both modern and old maps to detect outlines from shapes and boundaries, and boundary changes from one map to another, that relate to remains on the ground. He provides plenty of illustrations, including a windmill depicted by a rounded projection from the angle of a field, and a medieval deer park revealed by irregular boundaries where the fields are otherwise rectilinear. From older maps he reproduces a bowling green and a lost village. The emphasis is on both the detection of archaeological sites and the verification of those discovered by fieldwork and excavation. The methods seem to be looking for clues, such as part of the outline of a moat, or the deflection of a boundary around an obstacle that has since vanished, or deductions made about a group of shapes or boundaries.

However the value of these methods depends on the characteristics of those landscapes. Brown's experience was mainly in Leicestershire and Northamptonshire where straight boundaries are more prevalent, so the unusual is more noticeable. Kinks and deflections in field boundaries in other parts of the country, such as Lancashire, can have much more mundane origins, such as deflection around marl pits, quarries, ponds and waterlogged ground. Irregular boundaries can be due as much to minor watercourses concealed in hedgerows as to ancient boundaries in their own right. Christopher Taylor provided similar insights in Chapters Five and Six of his book *Fieldwork in Medieval Archaeology* looking at both the discovery and interpretation of sites using both printed documents and maps.[7] With modern maps he explores such themes as ponds as clues to medieval moats, deflections in rivers as clues to water-mills, isolated churches and other evidence that might explain references to settlement in documents. His use of older maps and plans is partly to support detection and partly to help elucidate detailed remains, once found.

This archaeological approach may be rewarding with the patience to follow up every clue, but in practice the proportion of kinks in field boundaries that produce windmill mounds or barrows or the foundations of early buildings are likely to be small return for the effort. Some of the effort can be provided by scrutiny of air photographs, and some by checking old maps and plans for plausible explanations of these kinks and irregularities. Similarly past buildings and structures on old maps and plans may be located on the modern map with the aid of both air photographs and fieldwork. Aerial photographs may reveal as crop and soil marks, or intermittent features, the courses of boundaries or the former presence of buildings. By cross-referring map and photograph a greater understanding of landscape evolution is possible.

As with fieldwork the local historian should perhaps take this a bit further. This is another medium where the question and answer approach is productive. By all means look for indicators of antiquities, but if such evidence is not forthcoming, look at old maps and plans as a resource for understanding the past landscape. The reason for including air photographs with old maps and plans is in order to make sufficient sense of the evidence. Some field and property boundaries on seventeenth- and eighteenth-century plans survive on present-day maps, but others have long since disappeared, or have been straightened or do not extend the previously indicated lengths. Using the early maps in conjunction with modern maps, vertical air photographs and fieldwork, look at how land management has changed from then until now, by trying to see the landscape as they saw it. Try to identify the reasons why buildings were placed in a given location, in terms of their function and any constraints there might have been, such as the limits of a property, or the contemporary practicalities of diverting water to a mill. Use the old maps in exactly the same way as Chapter Two suggested approaching fieldwork. The advantage of having vertical air photographs is to resolve incompatibilities between old and modern mapping, and to see clues in the landscape that the modern map may not show. The air photograph is a ready reference to explore spatial relationships that would take longer to explore on the ground, although ultimately it is no a substitute for direct observation.

Chapter Six

READING THE PHYSICAL LANDSCAPE

This is, I suppose, the physical geography chapter, and the one where some readers may protest that they picked up this book to enhance their history experience not to do geography. However, when we look at history on the ground we are also looking at the natural ground, which can confuse things, and which influences the way people utilise land. In particular it is easy to confuse natural and artificial landforms, and to distinguish natural components of artificially enhanced landforms.

Over the last two centuries we have become very successful at modifying the land surface to suit our needs, by cutting into hillsides, building embankments and tunnelling. We have also mastered the techniques of bridging obstacles, such as crossing rivers and ravines, or marshy ground. We are able to modify natural processes to reduce their impact. Our ancestors, before these times, mostly had to make the best of the landscape, and the impact of their land-shaping activities was more localised and less dramatic. Sometimes they could modify the landscape enough to make a difference, if there was sufficient justification, but mostly they adjusted their own lives around the landscape, sometimes hindered by it, but also sometimes able to take advantage of topography.

Hence when looking at the past the local historian needs to appreciate how the natural landscape helps and hinders. For example, agriculture is not simply about finding suitable soils for cultivation, but also managing soils, such as balancing the need to drain off surplus water or supplement sufficient moisture levels for agriculture by irrigation. Routeways are determined by practical considerations such as crossing boggy land, finding safe fording points on rivers, or cutting a terrace along a hillside. Where possible houses are built near where water can be found, on stable ground above seasonal flood levels and away from hazards like landslides. Watermills are constructed where sufficient head of water can be obtained. The local historian needs an appreciation of the physical landscape, to read it through the eyes of past settlers, to find the evidence of how they used it.

Archaeology and the natural environment

Archaeology texts often stress the importance of consulting geology and soil maps, for example Taylor (1974) and Brown (1987), but mysteriously these texts don't say what to do with them.[1] Bowden (1999) advocates 'some appreciation of the natural background of "solid" and "drift" geology must be achieved by anyone seeking to understand archaeological sites or landscapes' and also recommends 'a little research in a local library should provide adequate sources for the local geomorphology'.[2] Archaeologists often tell you the underlying geology when describing an archaeological site. It is not entirely clear why this should help interpretation. Modern archaeologists' concerns come out most strongly in a book aimed at making archaeology more accessible to schoolchildren, *Peopling Past Landscapes*, published in 1978.[3] This gives three reasons for studying the underlying rocks: the influence on settlement location, sources of building materials, and ancient trade routes. The evidence for trade routes hinges on finding alien stones: 'children rapidly learn to distinguish between a glacial erratic and a weathered piece of local stone'. They go on to say that children 'will get a thrill when the fragment of grey and honeycombed stone picked off the field surface turns out to be a piece of Niedermendig lava quarried for querns in the central Rhenish region from Roman times until the end of the Middle Ages.' Although the book explains the deficiencies in legibility and availability of one inch to the mile (1:63,360) geology maps, it doesn't explain what to do with them.

Peopling Past Landscapes does shed some light on the uncertainties of attributing soil characteristics to choice of settlement location. For example, the importance formerly attached to lighter and more permeable soils on chalk and limestone as locations for prehistoric settlement may simply be because these soils were less affected by agriculture until modern times, and evidence of prehistoric settlement has been ploughed out elsewhere. Similarly gravel terraces overlooking river valleys provided ideal contrast for air photo archaeology, but other areas were equally densely settled, just not so readily seen from the air. If anything that should alert archaeologists about the pitfalls of using soil maps, but again there is no guidance on how to interpret them. In spite of a mass of literature on environmental archaeology this is almost entirely directed at buried soils from the past and soil sections exposed in excavations. No-one seems prepared to explain why you need to study geology and soil maps in order to carry out field archaeology. It sometimes comes across as lip-service without any real comprehension.

One of the recurring justifications is the potential location of springs for water supply. However, while it is possible to predict where spring lines might occur from looking at a geology map, the causes are varied, and it is not a foolproof solution. A 1:25,000 scale topographical Ordnance Survey map (such as Explorer) may well provide this information, by indicating the location of wells and springs ('W' and 'Spr' in blue, accompanying a blue dot), and comparison with a geology map may then confirm the locus along which other springs may be found. It is also possible to identify springs in the field and determine the potential for others. Springs occur where permeable rock such as limestone or sandstone outcrops on a slope above impermeable rocks such as shale or slate. However the shale may be a thin band within a named strata that is otherwise permeable, and this information need not be obvious from a geological map. Artesian wells tap water trapped in porous rock between impermeable layers. Rainwater enters the porous rock where it outcrops, usually at a higher altitude, providing the head of water that enables it to rise to the surface through the assistance of a well shaft. Sometimes such trapped water finds a natural route to the surface, such as where obstructed by a fault or intrusion, and rises through cracks to appear as a spring. It would be difficult to predict such springs from a geology map.

The solid geology map will tell you the type of rock at or near the surface, and the drift geology maps will tell you about unconsolidated materials that mask the solid geology, such as boulder clay, peat or alluvium. You still need to know what such information signifies. The indicated rock type may be interspersed with clays, shales or gravels that give rise to local variations in soil type. Some labels are less informative, such as Reading Beds, Keuper Marls or Red Downtonian. A Geological Survey Memoir or Excursion Guide will go some way to answering these questions, but these resources are designed to help understand geology rather than human settlement patterns. Likewise a soil map and the accompanying soil survey guide or memoir will not facilitate finding settlements. Soil maps record the extent of soil series and associations, which are divided into subsets based on topography and other environmental factors. The accompanying guide will tell you the characteristics of the main soil on the map, and its variants, including underlying geology, drainage characteristics, and whether the soil is acidic or alkaline. However, as Aston observed 'the modern soil map may not reflect the situation 500, 1000, or more years ago.'[4] The climate was warmer and drier in Roman times, colder and wetter in the early medieval period, and during the Little Ice Age, from the fifteenth to the eighteenth century, winters were considerably colder and harsher than now. Pollution caused by industrial activity over the past hundred years has rendered rainwater in northern Europe significantly more acidic than normal, which in turn has made our soils more acidic. So again why do we need to look at soil maps?

Local historians and the physical landscape

There is currently a gap in the market for a guide to the physical landscape aimed at local historians and landscape archaeologists. In 1976 Collins published *A Guide to the British Landscape* by J.R.W. Cheatle (long since out of print), which this author found to be an invaluable pocket book to have around. It provided a compendium of the basics of every relevant discipline needed to understand the landscape, including geology, soils, geomorphology, vegetation, wildlife, agriculture, archaeology and architecture. Like any 'jack-of-all-trades' book, it didn't go into anything in much depth, but it was one of the few books I have ever encountered that provided just enough to fulfil most local historians' day-to-day needs. The section on the Geological Column described the composition of the main beds found on geology maps. The chapter on the physical evolution of the landscape provided essential insight on aquifers and spring lines. There was a simple explanation of the main soil types, and an illustrated classification of the main trees, shrubs, grasses and sedges. For example, Cheatle informs the reader that Cornbrash in the Jurassic (an exposure which can be traced from Yeovil in Somerset to beyond the Humber Bridge in South Yorkshire), is an aquifer often marked by a line of villages.[5]

For more detailed texts on geology, geomorphology and soils, it is important to remember that your reasons for consulting them are marginal, for the most part, to the reasons they were written, and their intended audiences. Therefore a basic textbook on geology, whether for students or popular science, is going to be mostly about structure, fossils and minerals rather than the where to find settlements. A useful guide to geology at the time of writing is Toghill (2000) *The Geology of Britain*, but it doesn't say much about the characteristics of the rocks for land use.[6] On soils a widely used educational textbook is by Ashman and Puri (2002), Essential Soil Science.[7] This is pitched at an appropriate level for schools, and provides good basic information that will mean something to local historians. Geomorphology texts tend to be complex, including mathematic models and elaborate theories, and the layman needs to browse a range of such books to find one or several to assist with the aspects relevant to local history. Again a school text book may be sufficient, although Huggett's *Fundamentals of Geomorphology* at undergraduate level is clear and concise.[8] The important subject matter for the local historian includes how rocks weather and disintegrate; the way materials move on slopes and accumulate at the foot of a slope; the mechanisms by which rivers erode and deposit sediments, and the effects of glacial and periglacial processes, which left their mark on the landscape of Britain during and after the last ice age. All of these processes affect the use of the landscape, the remains that survive, and can lead to misinterpretation of artificial landforms.

Soils depend upon the weathered rocks or drift deposits on which they develop, and the vegetation that grows on them, which provides and protects the organic component. Most British soils developed under extensive forests that evolved since the last ice age, and reached their peak about six thousand years ago. Since then these forests have been progressively cleared and replaced by cultivation, pasture and open heath or moor, perpetuated by human intervention such as managing grazing livestock and seasonal burning. An ideal cultivation soil in a UK context is a brown earth, which provides approximately a neutral pH of 7, and a rich soil fauna (including earthworms and bacteria) that quickly decomposes dead leaves and other organic matter into a brown gunge that is mixed in with the mineral soil. It also needs to have a suitable structure and texture. The ideal is a loam, which has a balance of clay and sand that allows easy root penetration but holds together sufficiently to allow water and air to fill the voids between the particles.

However many British soils are on heavy claylands that become hard to work in wet weather and are bone dry and cracked in summer, or sandy soils that do not hold water well and are easily carried by the wind. Likewise the ideal brown earth is not so common, not least because pollution has made our soils more acid. On more acid soils intense leaching, where rainwater passing through the soil dissolves essential nutrients, renders the upper soil poor. There is much less soil fauna, including few worms and no bacteria, so that decomposition relies more on fungal activity. Where soil is well drained, such as on sloping or undulating ground, this generally produces a podsol, where the upper profile is bleached not only of nutrients but of iron compounds and instead there is a concentrated iron-rich layer about a foot down, which impedes plant roots. The transition between the two includes a 'podsolized' brown earth. If drainage is poor, in low-lying ground such as a valley floor, and the water table fluctuates, rising into the active soil area, the soil is again poorer, and in extreme cases where permanently waterlogged, no decomposition takes place and peat accumulates. Again there are transitional stages including a gleyed brown earth. Cultivation is generally feasible between a podsolized brown earth and a gleyed brown earth. Where the underlying geology is chalk or limestone, the soil is too freely drained and often dries out, the soil tends to be mostly mineral with much organic matter being oxidised, and soils tend to be thin and less suited to cultivation, though good for grazing.

There are alternatives to just geology and soil maps as there is also a wealth of material on land-use history, such as the researches of Oliver Rackham, notably his *History of the Countryside*.[9] His books explore field systems, field boundaries, woodland and heathland. Other writers have followed on this tradition, such as Tom Williamson's *Shaping Medieval Landscapes*.[10] Others have prepared the way, for example, by analysis of pollen and other dating evidence in soil samples, to find out what was growing in the past, for example Petra Dark's *The Environment of Britain in the first millennium AD*.[11] Another useful exploration of changes since the last ice age, including the evolution of grasslands, is Ingrouille's *Historical Ecology of the British Flora*.[12] We know about past land use from documents, notably by means of detailed analysis of Domesday Book of 1086, such as H.C. Darby's study in 1977 which maps the distribution of arable, pasture, meadow and woodland.[13] We can also make retrospective deductions from modern land-use maps, such as the map sheets at 1:63,360 and 1:2,500 scale[14] and the regional volumes edited by Dudley Stamp, which show current distribution of arable, pasture, meadow and woodland. We can, at the very least, ask local farmers for their insights about the land they farm.

How to avoid confusing natural and artificial features

One thing that is unavoidable when looking at local history on the ground is the propensity for the natural landscape to present features easily confused as artificial. This is a much neglected subject, not least because the human modified landscape is less relevant to students of the physical landscape, such as the geologist and the geomorphologist. For them human factors may provide important clues, but mostly obscure or confuse the subject matter. On the other hand, those studying the human modified landscape may not give sufficient attention to misleading or confusing natural features. Yet the difficulties presented can be overcome by careful observation and background reading.

The best advice is to take care not to make obvious mistakes, which means looking out for alternative explanations. Covering every possible source of error would be time-consuming, and given the objective of increasing the corpus of knowledge of an area, small oversights cannot be avoided. Better to make sure that you have distinguished the obvious natural from the artificial components in a site, so you can respond should someone else, possibly an archaeologist, try to write off your efforts by casually attributing the evidence to natural causes.

The basic problem is that soil and vegetation frequently conceal the true character of features, both natural in origin and artificial. Also, over time, weathering and disintegration of remains can produce similar superficial appearances, even when devoid of soil and vegetation, that mean natural features can appear artificial. However there are ways of checking. As with the physical background to settlement and land use, this is knowledge which can be acquired progressively, by reading round the problems when the circumstances arise. The additional learning curve might deter local historians from embarking on fieldwork, but again some acquired and explored knowledge makes the local history more interesting. It may best be viewed as a trade off between the errors that might arise and the effort needed for risk avoidance.

Understanding geology

The two basic sources of error are geological formations that look artificial and where natural processes create landforms which look artificial (geomorphology). To establish the propensity for confusing geological features, this is when you need a geology map, for the structural information rather than composition (lithology). A 1:50,000 (or 1:63,630) scale geology map, while complex and detailed, may be sufficient for this purpose (although you may have to approach a university or college library rather than a public library to access one). In some localities, where the geology is an issue, it may be necessary to access 1:25,000 scale geology maps. If you need to purchase maps, the British Geological Survey publishes a small-scale 1:625,000 geology map which covers Britain in two sheets, north and south, which you may be able to find in a library. These are overprinted with a grid identifying the 1:50,000 scale map numbers and map titles if you need to purchase one. Alternatively you can get this information from the British Geological Survey online at www.bgs.ac.uk. If possible compare the geology map with a topographic map at the same scale (e.g. an Ordnance Survey 1:50,000 scale Landranger Map) to relate the contour information to the pattern of outcrops, as contour information is hard to see on the former. The geology map will reveal the pattern of outcrops of named stratigraphy, and the regional or local geology guide corresponding to the map, if one is available, will explain local variations within the stratigraphy.

What follows is a bit of a novelty, and wouldn't find a place in a geology textbook; however for local history on the ground this may be a viable innovation. I have identified four broad categories of structural geology which might affect the local historian's interpretation of features on the ground:

- Horizontal strata with few faults
- Dipping strata but still planar and with moderate faulting
- Folded and faulted structures
- All this complicated by intrusions and extrusions

There's a simple reason for making these distinctions. If you look at a geology map at 1:50,000 or better you should be able to determine, from the information below, whether the geology is going to make your fieldwork difficult. What is provided here is merely a guide. I strongly recommend getting a suitable geology textbook, such as Toghill (mentioned earlier) to explore the implications in more detail.

Horizontal strata

The map will provide some indication of this: a plus sign denotes horizontal. However there may be several cross-sections accompanying the map which will give an impression of the relationship of geological strata to the surface. Rock outcrops will follow the natural contour, or cross the contour very gradually if dipping slightly. On hillsides the outcropping rock will weather to varying degrees, sometimes forming a vertical face, and sometimes a steep slope covered in debris, and if fairly stable, concealed beneath soil and vegetation. This may also give rise to natural terraces or benches. Many parts of south-east England are like this, with either horizontal or gently dipping strata, particularly south-east of a line from Weymouth to the Wash.

Dipping strata

The symbol for this is an arrow accompanied by a number. The arrow shows the direction of true dip, and the number is the amount of dip in degrees away from the horizontal. True dip is perpendicular to the strike, which is the axis along which the top surface of the rock is horizontal, so sometimes the outcrop will be seen at an angle to the strike, in which case the perceived dip will be less than true dip. As before, cross-sections accompanying the geology map will help you visualise what is going on. Where there is dipping strata the rock outcrops will only follow the contour along the strike, as explained above, otherwise the outcrops will cross the contour at true dip or less. These relationships can be quite striking when a valley cuts through the strata. We tend to see such formations in a line from Weymouth to the Wash, along and parallel to the Jurassic Ridge.

Here there will be traps for the unwary fieldworker. The main rock types on the map are likely to include subordinate layers of differing resistance: clays, shales, sands and sandstones, silts and siltstones, bands of pebbles etc. Where rocks are steeply dipping, these may stand proud across hilltops or other more gradual surfaces. Where some of the rock layers are more actively weathered than others, they will appear as slots or trenches between the harder layers. Elsewhere the terraces or benches previously mentioned might appear like inclined terraced trackways. There is a risk of interpreting such an outcrop as a linear artificial feature, but these can be checked against the main patterns on the geology map.

Folded and faulted structures

Under tectonic processes the geology is subject to opposing forces which cause the strata to buckle upwards or downwards, as you would observe say, by pushing a table cloth from opposite sides, causing ridges to form. The cross-sections on a geology map are particularly useful to help visualise these effects, which can be quite difficult to read from the map. This is particularly so if erosion has removed the tops of the folds, or if the folds themselves are tilted along their long axis (plunging). Downward folds are referred to as synclines and upward folds as anticlines. Faulting of folded geology gives rise to an amazing variety of displacements and offsets. The pattern of outcrops can become very complicated, and there are a lot more features that can be confused with natural. However, careful checking of outcrop patterns on a geology map will help the fieldworker avoid obvious errors. It would be useful to go on some organised geology trips, if there is a local geological society or a university group organising such events, to become familiar with potential sources of error.

Intrusions and extrusions

The last category is where all the above are complicated by intrusive and extrusive volcanic rocks. These are usually found in a separate key on the margins of the geology map. They may represent large masses of magma which cooled at depth, but were subsequently exposed by erosion of the overlying sediments. Some molten material was squeezed up towards the surface through cracks, forming linear outcrops called dykes; between strata to form sheets called sills, and as localised features. Some molten rock was extruded and flowed over the land surface as lavas. This kind of geology contributes striking colours to geology maps, and is found mainly in Scotland, the Lake District, and parts of Wales and south-west England, and in north-west Ireland. Combined with intense folding and faulting the resulting geology is very complex. In such environments there is a high risk of encountering natural features that could be construed as artificial, and it is essential to look closely at the evidence. Find out if there is a local geology group that goes on field trips and get some first hand experience of local interpretation problems.

As I indicated earlier, this is an oversimplification, but I don't think geology is a big problem for local historians. The important thing is to look very carefully for live rock or naturally evolved concentrations of freestone when looking at the material composition of remains. Don't get caught by someone who comes to see what you have found and immediately points out that most of the remains you are interested in are a natural rock formation. On the other hand humans are generally lazy, and if nature has provided some upstanding material, why not incorporate that into a wall? It is only in very recent times that we have become preoccupied with sticking to straight lines in one direction, and either removing the rock or avoiding it.

This raises an important issue, however. There are a lot of sites where natural features have been used to advantage, and artificial construction has been minimal. Here there is a clear dichotomy between archaeology and local history. The lack of archaeology entailed in such constructions means there is limited excavation potential, and the irregularity of form prevents classification, so such sites are often ignored by archaeologists. It is also very easy for archaeologists to disregard sites with a lot of natural components. For local historians, adaptations of sites with limited need for artificial construction could still explain historical references. The fact that they have limited 'archaeological' content does not make them irrelevant. Plates 20 and 21 show the farmstead of Lassintullich near Kinloch Rannoch, Perthshire. With reference to Plate 20, east of the farm are two rocky elevations. To the right of the farm steading, the knoll with a visible terrace has the burial enclosure of the Stewarts of Inverhadden and the ruins of St Blane's Chapel. Above the steading the end of the rocky ridge, under an oak tree, has various 'rooms' cut out of the rock. Between them is a spring called St Peter's Well. According to A.D. Cunningham's *History of Rannoch* this was the site of a cell established by St Blane in the sixth century. This isn't archaeology, and it would probably be dismissed out of hand. Rock-cut spaces are neither classifiable nor archaeological. However this sort of site would greatly interest local historians. In fact there are a great many remains in the landscape which have too much natural composition, and which are not readily classifiable, which are ignored by archaeologists, but yet might tell us more about the past.

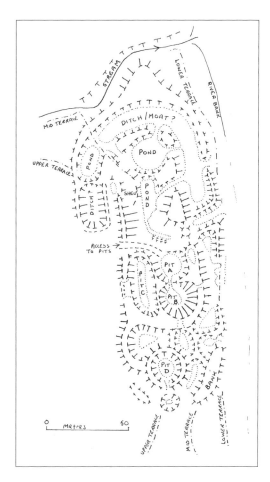

21 Auchingoul, near Bridge of Marnoch, Aberdeenshire. This rather complex pattern of ridges and hollows is traditionally believed to be an ancient camp, but because it is so difficult to interpret is nowadays classed as a quarry. Local historians and archaeologists think differently.

The same is true of sites where 'natural' is affected by quarrying or other modern disturbance. At Auchingoul, near Bridge of Marnoch, 12 kilometres north-north-east of Huntly in Aberdeenshire, there are some very strange remains in a wood on the banks of the River Deveron, at a key fording point (see Figure 21). On the opposite bank there is a part rock-cut part constructed hiding place known as Wallace's Camp, which is so well concealed it had been recorded for many years as lost. The remains in the wood were depicted on the 1882 Ordnance Survey 6 inch map as 'Camp (Supposed remains of)' but on more recent maps it is designated a quarry, and on the local Sites and Monuments Record it is attributed to quarrying and no longer considered significant. The remains are on three levels across three river terraces, but heavily pitted with small quarrying hollows with raised rims, and densely overgrown. In 1997 the writer spent three days trying to make sense of the remains, resulting in the complex sketchplan in Figure 21. Despite the almost unintelligible complexity, there is a curious symmetry to the site that makes it easy to understand the previous designation as a camp, and even the local tradition, improbable this far north, besides the unlikely shape, that it was a Roman camp. The lower northern part has a rounded end formed by a nearly continuous ditch; the southern part has distinctive enclosing banks, and the entrances east and west, the latter indicated by inturned banks, are symmetrically opposed. Despite my efforts the Archaeology Unit refused to reconsider the site as anything other than a quarry, and both the earthworks and Wallace's Camp remain 'non-archaeology'. Again, here is something which would interest local historians, but clearly doesn't interest archaeologists. However, archaeologists control what goes into the Sites and Monuments or Historic Environment Record, and what goes into published accounts. As a result a great deal of heritage goes unnoticed.

Understanding the geomorphology

Undoubtedly the greater interpretational problems lie with geomorphology, and yet these are least often explained in landscape archaeology texts. According to Bowden 'a little research in a local library should provide adequate sources for the local geomorphology.'[15] I suspect that our early ancestors, as they gradually developed artificial means of shelter and defence, made extensive use of natural features, not just caves and rock shelters, but natural mounds and ridges. It is thought that the embankments in the Dutch polders originated from mounds constructed as refuges in the event of floods, mimicking natural elevations that weren't always available where people chose to settle. Then someone had the bright idea to extend the mounds laterally to enclose spaces and keep out the rising waters. So the first defensive earthworks may simply have been used to fill the gaps where natural defences were inadequate. More sophisticated construction techniques followed over time, but when these deteriorated or collapsed the results were often little different from residual features left by natural processes. A lot of human-constructed landforms are basically just anthropological geomorphology. So I really think there's more to this than a little research in the local library, and my advice to local historians tackling local history on the ground is to worry more about the geomorphology than the geology.

The land surface is not merely soil overlying weathered rocks. On slopes the soil and the weathered mantle below it are inclined to move under gravity, either slowly as creep, or more dramatically as landslips and mudflows. In early post-glacial times freezing and thawing of the subsurface produced flow structures known as solifluction lobes, and where these meet the valley floor they sometimes form terraces. Some of these formations on slopes can be confused as artificial. Remains of structures on slopes are distorted by movements below, as well as on the surface, causing them to overturn and tumble. Weathered rock outcrops produce a cast of broken material which carried downslope can produce stony alignments that are natural rather than artificial. On steeper slopes soil creep produces numerous steps due to vertical slippage, rather than a continuous surface, giving the appearance of small diverging terraces. Objects are transported downslope by surface wash during heavy rain, and carried in slowly creeping soils. At the slope foot this moved material accumulates as colluvium. Colluvium also buries remains of settlements and other human activities that hugged the slopefoot for shelter. There may be signs of remains passing under the colluvium at the present slope base.

An interesting illustration of the interpretational problems is the relationship of human settlement to alluvial fans. These occur, especially in upland areas, where gullies and ravines are formed by torrents of water after heavy rain or snow melt. Where these torrents emerge on a valley side, a fan or cone of stones and mud is formed. Those of a more stony composition probably date back to early post-glacial or were more active during the Little Ice Age (sixteenth to eighteenth centuries). Their current seasonal downwash is closer to the central axis of the fan, and the outer edges of the fan are more stable. The fan margins attract settlement because the materials are more amenable to excavating terraces for houses, finding freestone for building, and in the process making use of ground unsuited to cultivation. Also the settlers have ready access to water from the stream. However, during harsher conditions, such as during the Little Ice Age, large outpourings of rocks and sediment occasionally engulfed the houses. It is sometimes possible to find remains of these houses from their built-out downslope edges, where the upslope part is buried. The author has found some very good examples of this in Sutherland, where the engulfed settlements are shown live on early maps such as Roy's Military Survey 1747–55.[16] Figure 22 shows Pairc a' Chlaigann, in Rhidorroch Forest near Ullapool. The mudlow fronts are demarcated by a line of Ts, and the house sites by letters A–K; the upslope sides of the houses are buried under mud, so they appear on the ground like staples. In the 1990s there was an interesting collaboration of an archaeologist (Stratford Halliday of the Royal Commission in Scotland) and a geomorphologist Richard Tipping.[17] The archaeologist contributed to the environmental archaeology (radiocarbon dating and pollen analysis), and also observed the relationships between archaeology, such as cultivation terraces and ridge-and-furrow patterns, and the re-activation of alluvial fans. The converse application of geomorphology to archaeology in relation to understanding settlement on and near alluvial fans is less often apparent.

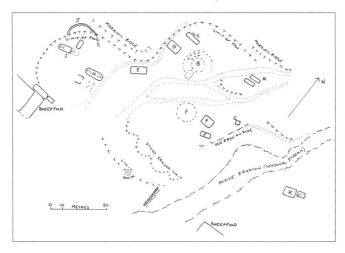

22 Pairc a' Chlaigann, near Ullapool, Wester Ross – eighteenth-century settlement partly buried by mudflow. The ground rises northwards, parallel to the boulder-strewn watercourse.

Another important geomorphological process to consider is mass movement, which includes flows where the slope materials achieve liquid characteristics, slides and slips. One of the flow characteristics is creep, where small laminations slide over each other or such layers distort and overturn, a process often revealed by trees (see Plate 22, which shows trees on the march in Rhidorroch Forest, near Ullapool in Wester Ross). Consider the distortion effect this can have on any archaeological remains, together with the accumulation of material at the slope foot (colluvium). Depending on the underlying geology, the amount of moisture present, and the gradient of slopes, some sudden mass movements are planar, parallel to the slope. Others are rotational, where the slip plane is curved, and the slipped mass rotates, creating detached elevations. In some areas, such as in the Peak District, if the mass has remained fairly stable in recent times you can find minor settlement remains on the ridge formed by the rotational mass. However there needs to be greater understanding of mass movement in archaeology, as these processes also affect artificial structures. For example Figure 23 shows Clifford Hill near Northampton, where terraces on the south side have been attributed to a landslip. However on a conical mound the displacements and scars would be very different, and they probably derive from earlier phases in the construction of the motte. It has also been suggested that the rectangular area south of the mound, M on Figure 23, was formed from the upcast created by recutting the ditch after the landslip, whereas traces of linear ditches either side correspond to the ditch east and west of the mound, suggesting a moated site here before the mound was constructed.

A very worthwhile resource for the local historian concerned about understanding the physical landscape is Ballantyne and Harris (1994) *The Periglaciation of Great Britain*.[18] This explains many phenomena associated with glaciation and the early post-glacial period in the British landscape, backed by illustrations of relic features in Britain, and present-day features in Northern Europe and Canada. Importantly they provide maps of the distribution of these phenomena in Britain, and where they are most likely to be found. They cover some very important subject matter such as ice wedges, frost polygons and patterned ground, which can have considerable impact on air photo archaeology, and can also generate misleading features on the ground. They explore slope-forming processes and the explanations of various natural mounds and banks. Whilst designed for the enthusiastic periglacial geomorphologist, it is a handy reference for the landscape historian wary of making mistakes.

Depending on how far you want to get involved, a little precautionary reading and observation will suffice if you only want to dip your toe into local history on the ground; however if you are serious about it, you need to take on as much as you feel will help you make the right decisions. Periglacial features are particularly important to air photo archaeology, because these seem only vaguely understood. I referred in Chapter Five to Wilson's *Air Photo Interpretation for Archaeologists* which devotes seventeen pages to confusing natural features; however the range and complexity of periglacial features that can affect archaeological interpretation justifies a book on the subject rather than part of a chapter. A supposed henge at Dallington, near Northampton, besides including sloping ground, is the composite of two frost polygons, and their contribution was clearly visible as lines of shattered stone when bike scramblers invaded the site.

A very good example of where greater understanding of a phenomenon is necessary is the 'pingo'. A revolutionary text in 1978, John Evans' *An Introduction to Environmental Archaeology* had a chapter on 'Natural Situations'.[19] This covered a wide range of topics in very few pages culminating in a description of pingos. The explanation given was accurate, but there was nothing said about location, and the term 'pingo' cropped up everywhere in archaeological literature in the ensuing

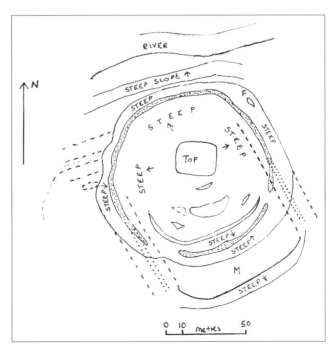

23 Clifford Hill, near Northampton. Are terraces here caused by a landslip or do they represent earlier phases of construction? Geomorphology is seldom understood in archaeology.

decades. For example, in Brown's *Fieldwork for Archaeologists and Local Historians*, he has a section on natural features that can be confused with artificial:[20]

> Another legacy of the ice age is the pingo, the result of the forcing upwards and subsequent melting of large cones of ice; they leave behind sometimes perfectly circular depressions with earth banks around them which look like hut circles, pond barrows or bomb craters.

The phenomenon may date back to Taylor in 1974: 'pingos or collapsed ice mounds can also form circular depressions with an apparent "rampart" around them which might cause confusion.'[21] Pingos are mainly found in south-west Wales (particularly Dyfed), East Anglia and the Thames basin, around the limits of the late Devensian ice sheet, though they have been found in southern Cumbria and the Isle of Man.[22] They haven't been found in north-east England or Scotland and are rare outside the three main locations. They are irregular ovals rather than perfectly circular, as they tend to occur on gently sloping ground at the edge of valley floors and near spring lines, which may have been a factor in their formation. The depressions are 10 to 120 metres in diameter and up to 3 metres deep.[23] Sometimes ploughed-out ones can be seen on air photographs. They often occur in clusters which interlock suggesting successive generations. There are a variety of ramparted depressions produced in periglacial environments, and some of them can look like fortifications, so the risk of confusion is something to take seriously. But one wonders how many genuine hut circles and pond barrows have ended up classed as pingos in unlikely locations.

The important point to make here is that most natural landforms have characteristics that can be used to identify them. They occur in recognisable contexts and associations. The issue of confusing natural and artificial features need not be the impenetrable mystery, known only to an elite of experts, it is sometimes made out to be. The main difficulty for the local historian exploring the landscape is when the amount of effort in recognising false clues outweighs the pleasure of exploring. The advantage the local historian has, however, is that in one locality, the natural phenomena can be learned about. This might be achieved by joining a geology group for a while, to get to know the main features of local area landscapes. The problem is more of an issue for those travelling around to do fieldwork: each area visited then presents new interpretational problems. What this chapter has endeavoured to explain is that there are ways of finding out, and this need not be onerous (though may be a little bit more than a little research in the local library). Finding out about sources of confusion in the landscape also helps understand the landscape that confronted past peoples. In that sense reading the physical landscape is just as important a task as reading the past in the landscape.

Chapter Seven

ROMAN ROADS AND OTHER LONG LINES

Having spent so much of this book dwelling on the problems of interpretation of remains it is impossible to avoid one of the most contentious: Roman roads. Not all Roman roads are contentious perhaps, but there are Roman attributions to roads in almost every parish. If not a Roman road, then some other kind of ancient track, or perhaps an ancient boundary bank forming an ancient defence, or the boundary of some ancient territory. In short, this chapter is about long linear earthworks of one kind or another, but the ubiquitous Roman road is a good cover-all for a difficult subject area that most local historians will encounter. The moral dilemma is perhaps most effectively described by Christopher Taylor:[1]

> Perhaps the greatest problem in the understanding of roads lies in the minds of those who wish to unravel their history. The fascination of roads and tracks, and the excitement that the process of tracing them onwards across country gives, have all too often in the past resulted in complete mental blocks and visual blindness. The same situation unfortunately still exists today. The desire to trace a line of communication, any line, to a significant point, any point, and to clothe it with romantic visions of prehistoric farmers, Roman soldiers or medieval travellers leads to greater and greater flights of fancy and in the end total nonsense.

Taylor, here, was expressing disapproval of the works of Alfred Watkins and successive acolytes who trace thousands of straight roads radiating from every conceivable focal point on the landscape.[2] A simpler response to this is that the laying out and maintenance of tracks is a labour-intensive activity that probably led to very few rather than many tracks being laid, and you reach a point, with straight track enthusiasts, where there is no ground left on which to cultivate, let alone to live and breath. The ease with which you can find common alignments over 10 or 20 kilometres distance ought to be perceived as a warning that this has more to do with chance than reality. However, while not disagreeing with

Taylor's concerns about straight track enthusiasts, the same cautions need to be applied to Roman roads and other alignments. Alfred Watkins and his followers are not the only culprits when it comes to inventive and improbable alignments. A similar observation to Taylor's can be found in Aston:[3]

> A great deal of rubbish has been written in the past about roads, particularly Roman roads and ridgeways. It has been all too easy in the long winter evenings to sit down in an easy chair in front of the fire with a 1-inch (now 1:50000) Ordnance Survey map and draw in straight sections of roads, paths and parish boundaries, and suggest possible and probable road links across the landscape. Little attention is paid to why a particular road might have gone this way or that, what it is used for and which settlements it was linking.

Again this is sensible advice, and one that springs to mind as I sit through episodes of *Time Team*. Neither Taylor nor Aston make sufficient distinction, in the way they describe these activities, between straight track hunters and countless others making genuine attempts to explore alignments. Nor do they make sufficient distinction between what professional archaeologists do themselves, and those, by implication amateurs, whom they castigate. It is not that looking for alignments on maps is taboo, but that the alignments have to make sense, in terms of how past peoples used the landscape. These quotations might better serve as a caution to all, but I wish they had been worded less judgmentally by their authors.

Avoiding the pitfalls

As a consequence, tracing Roman roads, or any other alignments, is perceived as eccentric. This is most unfortunate, as the process of such investigations is a thoroughly good way of getting to grips with understanding landscapes. Communications are important elements of any landscape, and the way these communications utilise the landscape, to surmount or avoid obstacles, helps to explain the pattern of settlement and economic activity. This becomes particularly important if the topography creates bottlenecks due to gaps in high ground, skirting marshland or utilising fording points on rivers, as settlement locations will generally fall in line. If these routeways are not immediately obvious, then finding them can often be a first step in understanding a local landscape. This is best achieved by combining fieldwork, map work and documentary research. As long as certain precautions are observed, searching out routeways can be a rewarding and respectable pursuit.

Sometimes well intended advice has been taken too literally. In the introduction to Margary's *Roman Roads in Britain* is this advice regarding hedgerows:[4]

> Hedgerow lines, sometimes of considerable length, and lanes or minor roads, with footpaths and tracks, often mark part of the course and are very significant if a long line can then be traced across country, even when in discontinuous lengths upon the same alignment.

Taken too literally this can have the same consequences as searching for alignments on maps, because over a distance of several kilometres entirely unrelated alignments can readily be found. Such evidence should only be used to connect proven lengths of road. Another problem lies with attempts to interpret linear concentrations of stones or stony ground as road metalling. Margary warns about surface diggings for stone that follow an outcrop and dumps of stone collected off the field alongside field boundaries.[5] However too many roads have been 'traced' relying solely on stoniness in ploughed fields or showing through grass. Margary 421 passes about five kilometres north of Portsmouth, having until Bedhampton followed the modern A27 from Chichester, and thereafter strikes across open county to Wickham en route to Bitterne, near Southampton. Margary says that it is visible on Lye Heath, and in 1973 there was a rescue excavation, ahead of the laying of a water main, where it crossed the Roman road at SU 647086.[6] In 1985, when I explored this road, after a crop of maize had been harvested, there were two sinuous outcrops of flint gravel across the field, one coinciding with the excavation.[7] Ideally, Roman road excavations should include several small excavations in proximity to check for other causes, but invariably the excavation is a narrow window confined to the road alignment. The danger is all too apparent with the example of Margary 151. This road leaves Stane Street (Margary 15) at Rowhook, just north of the posting station at Alfoldean,[8] bound for the Roman site at Farley Heath and thought to join Margary 4a near Bagshot. The evidence for the road relies on 'abundant remains of the metalling, mainly chert and ironstone, with flint and pebbles, too, especially towards the Rowhook end, which are plainly traceable upon the stoneless soil of a very heavy clay.' However this heads directly for a very steep hillside, at Winterfold House TQ 074420, two kilometres north-west of Ewhurst, a little to the east of a steep dry valley, where it supposedly negotiates a one in three gradient. Slightly different alignments could have found easier ascents.

There are two ways to avoid over-reliance on limited evidence. One is to check for variations at frequent intervals; the other, as already demonstrated in Chapter One, with Tun Brook near Preston, is to look at obstacles to the alignment and the options for overcoming them. When following any alignment, whether an old road or a linear earthwork, checks should be made at frequent intervals. When following ruinous banks through scrubby woodland or very faint remains in open ground, checks might need to be as frequent as every 10 metres, whereas for more reliable remains in good conditions every 30 metres might suffice. Ideally these should be offsets from a baseline, either following an existing mapped boundary or referenced to mapped coordinates, so that the evidence can be plotted.

As suggested in Chapter Four, look for consistency of construction, and relationship to other features, especially those that come into contact or cross the line. Also look at how the remains adapt to or modify the natural topography. Roman roads usually have some impact on the landscape, cutting a terrace across a slope or building on a firm foundation, with a camber to enhance drainage, commonly described by Roman road hunters as an 'agger'. At each checkpoint look for changes in the condition and construction and examine any potentially misleading features either side. Linear features are often re-used as local boundaries, so there may be several phases of construction on some lengths. Sometimes the original feature being followed is reduced to scant remains while a later adaptation strikes off on a different alignment. Hence regular checks can pick out any divergences from the alignment thought to be original, and backtracked to the point where they diverge. For road or linear earthwork enthusiasts tracking remains over long distances, such caution may be considered too laborious, but for the local historian, who may only be investigating a local feature over a few kilometres, careful plotting may be well worth the effort.

Tun Brook, Preston provides a rather extreme case of the obstacle problem, which can range from how roads cross small streams or broad rivers, boggy ground, slopes prone to landslips, or gullies of any shape or size. The Tun Brook investigation was part of an exploration of all the obstacles on Margary 703, which was supposed to extend from Ribchester to Poulton le Fylde, but probably only got as far as Kirkham.[9] The road might have benefited from a more southerly route west of Preston, making use of easier crossings of intervening valleys, but there was no more reliable evidence of the road on this route than on the original. It was a problem-solving exercise, such as was explained in Chapter Two, whereby all the possible options used over time should be considered, to see how not only the Romans, but people up until the present time, adapted or circumnavigated obstacles to communication. It is one of the best ways of getting to understand a locality.

The author had two early experiences of the trials and tribulations of tracking Roman Roads. One was an alternative to Long Causeway in South Yorkshire in the latter half of the 1970s; the other was the enigma of the Devil's Highway, in Surrey and Berkshire, in the early 1980s, where the course of the original earthwork is at odds with the mapped road. In both cases the author was unable to change the status quo, although more than thirty years on, Long Causeway has been discounted as a Roman road, and the author's alternative is beginning to be considered by others. These experiences illustrate many of the difficulties likely to be encountered, not least that however rewarding the pursuit of alignments can be, it takes more than a lifetime to change anything in archaeology. That shouldn't stop local historians exploring their own 'Roman roads'. However, what I want to show, though these examples, is how difficult it is to achieve change. The local historian may have to be content with less auspicious outcomes, such as adding to the possibilities in the landscape, and improving understanding. That perspective is not intended to discourage the local historian from fieldwork along old roads, which I hope they will pursue and enjoy. The object is to provide insight into the necessary precautions and pitfalls that can be encountered, which will hopefully equip local historians to venture forth undeterred.

Long Causeway – avoiding obstacles

Like Tun Brook, Stanage Edge, north of Hathersage in the Peak District, is another barrier (Figure 24). The most northerly of a series of gritstone cliffs that extend down the eastern valley edge of the River Derwent as far as Chatsworth, they are popular with rock climbers. Eastwards from these edges are large tracts

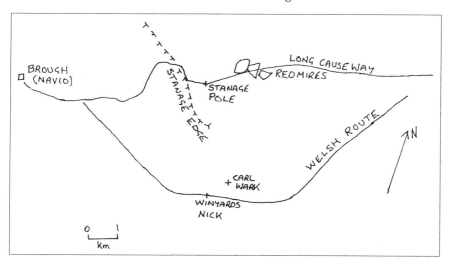

24 Long Causeway and 'Welsh' road routes. Modern routes use the gap two kilometres south of Winyards Nick, in the gap between Stanage Edge and Froggat/Curbar Edge. The shortest route between Templeborough and Navio is via Redmires, whereas the apparent Roman road traced by the writer makes a long detour south to take advantage of the easier gradients between the edges.

of moorland. There are few breaks in this frontier, and one of the most important is where the edges are offset by faulting, and dissected by streams, in and around Burbage Brook and Nether Padley, to the east of Hathersage. This forms a sizeable gap between Stanage Edge and the equally forbidding Froggatt Edge. The gap today accommodates the main routes linking Sheffield to the Derwent Valley. So if a Roman road was to cross the moors from the Roman fort at Templeborough, near Rotherham, through Sheffield to the fort at Brough on Navio, near Hope, in the Derwent Valley, the next fort due west, what is the logical route it would follow? Why, straight over Stanage Edge of course: Margary 710b known as 'Long Causeway' ploughs straight through a succession of obstacles better suited to testing tanks.[10] My involvement started by fortuitous accident.

On the western fringe of Sheffield is the small hamlet of Ringinglow, on the boundary of the Peak District National Park. Whereas Ringinglow Road continues westwards, around the head of Burbage Brook, branching south-west at Ringinglow is an old turnpike road across Houndkirk Moor to Fox House Inn. This old road is a popular route for walkers. By tradition it is known as 'Roman Road', though that was something I found out later, and it is an attribution to an old straight road rather than for any real antiquarian reason. Unfortunately these attributions are often scoffed at by experts, when they should be looked into with greater care.

What drew me out to Ringinglow in late 1975 and early 1976 were some features I had seen on aerial photographs, crossing Houndkirk Moor on a slightly different path from the old turnpike. The features were first brought to my attention by a third-year undergraduate in a remote sensing class in which I was

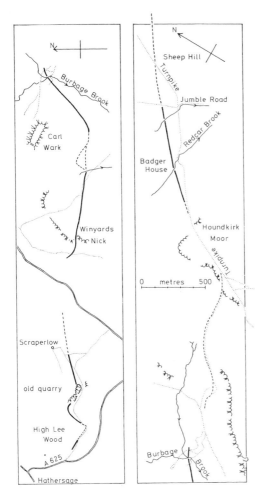

25 Route of road remains across Burbage and Houndkirk Moors Sheffield. This overall view of the route traced by the writer was previously published in the *Yorkshire Archaeological Journal* Vol. 50 1984.

assistant, who was doing a project with the photographs concerned. The heather moor here is frequently prone to fire, whether intentional or accidental, and one such fire, several years earlier, had exposed a cambered road, with kerb stones and side ditches. Starting at Copperas House, it crosses the south-east corner of Lady Canning's Plantation, and continues towards a ruined steading known as Badger House. About 400 metres south-west of Badger House this cambered road merged with the turnpike for about 600 metres, then struck westwards towards Burbage Brook (see Figure 25 & Plate 23). It crosses the brook and ascends south-west, turning to cross the moor to Winyards Nick, a notch in the crags overlooking Hathersage. Either side of Winyards Nick the camber had been deeply eroded by old trackways. It then descended to the Derwent Valley near Hathersage.[11] The crossing of Burbage Brook was particularly unusual: an inclined terraceway rising from what appeared to have been a substantial bridge crossing Burbage Brook (Plate 24). The bridge was approached from the west by an inclined track in a hollow way which emerged on a causeway or abutment 20 metres long, which had been cut through twice by a zigzag track using the hollow way. This was followed by apparent stumps of bridge piers and an abutment on the east bank. Being eroded into and crossed by so many later tracks this looked like a very old road (Figure 26).

What I had found was a series of disconnected lengths of a cambered roadway, which fitted the description of a Roman agger, but which were so closely interwoven with the system of early turnpikes and pack ways that crossed the moors here, that there was little hope of convincing anyone of a Roman origin. However as a route which avoided Stanage Edge it did seem to make sense that this might be the Roman road from Templeborough to Navio. The reaction, from almost every quarter, was that all I was doing was making connections between entirely unrelated lengths of late medieval and post-medieval routeways. Both Aston and Taylor's warnings spring to mind here, and I was doubly careful with every observation. Another counter-argument was that the recognised route of Long Causeway was a lot nearer a straight line between the two forts than my southwards peregrination (Figure 24).

I was faced with a two-fold problem that confronts anyone who tries to discover new Roman roads or other linear earthworks: it looked convincing to me, but I couldn't convince anyone else; indeed I couldn't get anyone else to come out and look with me. Amazingly quickly the 'straight track' label puts you at a distance from professionals and 'serious' amateurs. I was convinced I could see a consistent feature: a cambered road with a metalled surface, kerbs and side ditches, of the right width and appearance to be identified as a Roman road. I

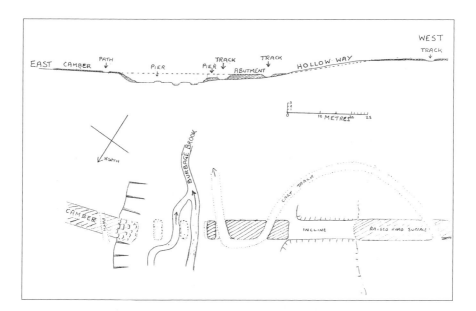

26 Plan of possible Roman bridge crossing Burbage Brook, a drawing in 1976. No-one disputed that it was a bridge, but everyone disputed that it was anything older than eighteenth century.

was also certain it was different from more obviously post-medieval counterparts along the way. These were rough metalled benches built out from the slope, with a drystone wall supporting on the downslope side, or narrower 'causeways' paved with slabs, intended as routes for pack animals. The trouble is, there are post-medieval roads which are cambered, kerbed and have side ditches, and I could not prove that I wasn't just looking at examples of such roads intermeshed with the other road building styles on the moors. I was 25 when I found my road, still full of ideals and indignation at having my beliefs dismissed. The opposition included Sheffield University Department of Archaeology and the Hallamshire Archaeological Society, both steadfast supporters of Long Causeway. It was not an argument I had any hope of winning.

At the time the accepted course of the Roman road crossed Sheffield and followed close to Redmires Road to Lodge Moor, and through the reservoirs there to Stanedge Pole, on the boundary between South Yorkshire and Derbyshire. From there it approached Stanage Edge, which it gradually descended in a long sweeping curve to a spot called Dennis Knoll, to the north of Hathersage (Figure 24). Between Redmires Reservoir and Stanage Edge there was a distinct causeway of large slabs, narrower than a Roman road, and more typical of a packhorse route, and it appears on Jeffrey's Map of 1771 as a cartway from Stannington to Hathersage, known in the nineteenth century as Long Causeway.[12] Its Roman origin was first suggested by J.D. Leader in 1877[13] and a description was published in Guest's *History of Rotherham* in 1879.[14] Hence it is described in Codrington's *Roman Roads in Britain*[15] in 1918 and in Margary's book of the same title in 1955 as Route 710b.[16] By the time of my own discovery this was the established Roman road, despite its precarious descent of Stanage Edge.

Over the intervening years the Long Causeway route over Stanage Edge has lost credibility and is no longer considered to be Roman in origin.[17] It doesn't follow that my route takes its place. The principle is that there is a Roman road between Templeborough and Navio, just the route is unknown; maybe one day a professional archaeologist will rediscover my route and it will take its rightful place. I have had supporters, for which I am grateful, and to whom I owe what visibility I can hang on to, such as the 1980 edition of *Peakland Roads and Trackways*,[18] and more recently the route was the subject of a dissertation by a local archaeologist.[19] However, in the intervening years, I was able to build on later experience of other Roman roads. I progressed my skills in checking, by means of transects and offsets, scrutinising every section for signs of alignment changes where I might have misconstrued continuity, and ensuring that the camber with its stone kerbs and side ditches was consistent in every detail. I researched the history of post-medieval routeways to ensure that there was no more recent explanation.

One thing the Sheffield road did provide was the opportunity to explore 'stratigraphy' as applied to the sequence of coincident features, discussed in Chapter Four. In the process of investigation, I had to try to establish whether my road remains were later or earlier than the other road remains that shared parts of the route. The best illustration of this was at Winyard's Nick, a notch in the gritstone edges overlooking Hathersage. Right up to the present day this has been used as a routeway, approached in either direction by a fan of trackways,

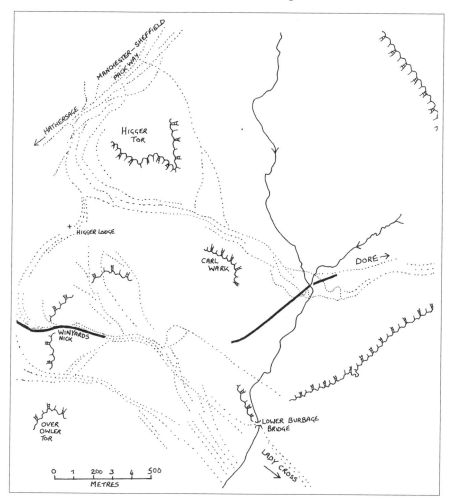

27 Plan of the writer's road approaching Winyards Nick. This sketch plan from the early 1980s is based on an air photograph. It shows how the road remains fitted in with the network of trackways, and shows both the crossing of Burbage Brook, with its south-westward incline, across the grain of other trackways, and the route through Winyards Nick.

and deeply worn down by the tread of many feet (Figure 27). Today the nick is about six metres deep, but at the time my road was laid through the gap it was only two metres deep. Subsequent traffic has eroded the north side of my road, leaving the southern edge of the camber, kerb and ditch hanging on the side of the nick. The remains of several successive medieval pathways also survive as lower terraces and fragments on the sides of the nick (Plate 25). One was a hollow way, the second, at an even lower level, was typical of a pack-horse causeway. Modern traffic has worn the floor a metre below that. With careful fieldwork I explored how the different routeways approached and exited Winyard's Nick to show the stratigraphy. However it was to no avail. Twenty-four years on, my 1984 publication of this analysis is every bit as unknown as the road itself.[20]

My account of my alternative route to Long Causeway is not here to put local historians off trying to pursue their own Roman roads. Quite the opposite, I'm determined by writing this chapter to encourage local historians to get out there and look because my own thesis is that understanding communications is crucial to understanding landscapes. However I hope that by describing my experiences I have highlighted the potential pitfalls and the difficulties in challenging established ideas. You need to explore all the questions highlighted in Chapter Four in order to avoid 'flights of fancy'. So my second illustration is important to show just how bizarre things can get in the Roman road debate.

The Devil's Highway: remains or invisible straight lines?

My quest for the road known as Margary 4a, between London and Silchester, westwards of Staines, was again about alternatives, but in this case I was looking for an earthwork described in the eighteenth and nineteenth centuries, which may or may not be the Roman road. The earthwork has been known for centuries as the Devil's Highway. According to an early description it was 'raised with a trench on each side of it, and not less than ninety feet wide', and another observer reported it to be eight feet high.[21] From about 1821 engineer cadets at Sandhurst were engaged in surveys to assist the researches of Wyatt Edgell of Egham, a local antiquary, who was trying to locate the Roman town of Pontes at Staines.[22] Some of the plans they produced are preserved at the Royal Military College Museum at Sandhurst, though mostly of features to the north of Sandhurst. Figure 28 shows the writer's impression of the course of the linear earthwork in relation to the official Roman road line (Margary 4a).

Unfortunately the RMC plans for the continuation from Dukes Hill, north of Bagshot, to Staines do not seem to have survived, but their description of the route was published in the *United Services Journal* and *Gentleman's Magazine* in 1836.[23] In 1854 Colonel McDougal of RMC Sandhurst presented a paper on the subject to Surrey Archaeological Society, and in the following year this was published with a plan executed by McDougall.[24] This shows the Roman road as two straight lines with a change of direction at Duke's Hill near Bagshot, which formed the basis of all later descriptions, including Codrington's account and Margary 4a.[25] However McDougal reproduced the 1836 descriptions, which do not appear to describe the same route. Somewhere in the interval the principle that all Roman roads are straight had taken precedence.

What we have here are descriptions of a large earthwork that was visible more than 170 years ago, and what may be a completely separate entity, as things gradually turned out, the Roman road between London and Silchester. Greater understanding of the conflicting accounts can be gleaned from the following extract from the 1836 version, describing the course of the Roman road between Sunning Hill Road and Virginia Water.

From the Sunning Hill Road it crosses some low meadow land where it can scarcely be discerned; and at about a mile from this spot, where it enters

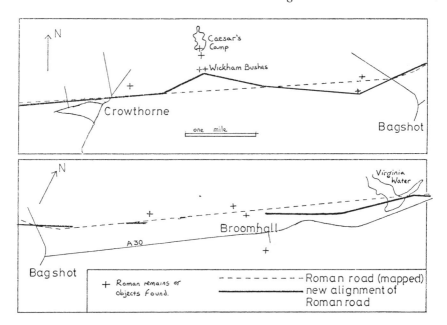

28 The linear earthwork in relation to Margary 4a. This shows the author's route between Crowthorne and Virginia Water as published with an article in a company magazine (EASAMS, once part of GEC).

Windsor Park, it is for awhile totally lost. There is however a portion in good preservation between the point where it enters the Park and the place where its line of direction cuts Virginia Water; it can also be distinguished in a spot near the Belvidere between these two points, where one of the Park rides runs for about three hundred yards along the top; and the labourers assert that this part of the ride having never required any repair, they had from thence been led to conclude that it was constructed on some ancient road. It should be remarked that the part of the Virginia Water which is crossed by the direction of the Roman road is artificial, and has been formed only within the last forty years.

From this spot the direction of the road is through the yard of the Inn at Virginia Water; and there is a tradition that the foundation had lately been discovered there. Lastly, at Bakeham House, situated in the same line of direction, on the brow of the hill which forms the east end of the elevated plain called Englefield Green, the substratum of the road, the foundations of a tower or other strong building, with a variety of Roman remains, have been discovered within the last few months.

McDougall's account in 1855 provides the same information with slight changes of wording, though still saying Virginia Water was formed within the last forty years (nearer sixty in 1855). However the map is perplexing. It clearly crosses Shrubbs Hill just north of the present A30 (at SU 962676), which is shown with the junction with Bedford Lane. It passes close to the rides in the woods south-east of Fort Belvedere, but then runs through the outlet of

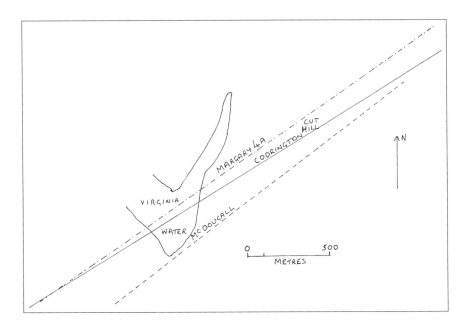

29 Different interpretations of the Roman Road crossing Virginia Water. It isn't easy to represent these Roman road alignments from descriptions, but it shows the three 'authorities' did not agree.

Virginia Water (SU 977686), crosses the A30 at the junction with Christchurch Road, by the Wheatsheaf Hotel, and through Clock Case Woods to the south of the London Road (see Figure 29). This is a straight line locally, but extended westwards it diverges southwards of the supposed line to Dukes Hill. In short there is something wrong with McDougall's cartography. For McDougall's map to be accurate, there would have to be additional direction changes in the Roman road. Hence later commentators were understandably perplexed. This is from Codrington's account in 1903; he is describing the road westwards from London:[26]

> Beyond Bakeham the memoir referred to states that the course was through the yard of the inn at Virginia Water, where according to a tradition a foundation of gravel, supposed to be the Roman road, had formerly been discovered; and also the line cuts Virginia Water, and that the ridge could be distinguished for 300 yards, where one of the drives in Windsor Forest ran along it. The yard of the inn seems to be out of line across any part of Virginia Water, and no trace of the ridge is now visible on to Belvedere, and the course of the road is uncertain.
>
> It is likely that the hill on which the Belvedere Tower stands (260') was the point made for from Bakeham Hill, though it was perhaps avoided by the road.

If the road runs from Bakeham Hill towards the Belvedere Fort, the alignment now crosses Virginia Water some 200 metres north of the outlet, where McDougall showed it to cross, and would lie north of the London Road on Cut Hill, again until about a kilometre north-east of where McDougall's map shows it cross (Figure 29). Margary, on the other hand, avoids the complications.[27]

> The line of the road is visible again at Sunningdale, where a distinct agger follows a hedgerow line from the cross-roads opposite the church to Rise Road, a very substantial affair 24 feet wide and metalled with gravel. It can be faintly seen crossing low ground north-east of the church towards Fort Belvedere, where a woodland ride is said to follow it for 300 yards. This line points to Bakeham House, as has been said, cutting through the valley now occupied by Virginia Water, which is however, an artificially embanked lake. By an odd freak of chance it would have reached the lake just at the point where the transplanted Roman columns and other relics from Cyrene in North Africa were set up many years ago, a trap for the unwary beginner in archaeology!

Margary's route, shown on modern maps, is consistent with the alignment from Duke's Hill, Bagshot, but passes through the Belvedere Fort (Figure 29). It crosses Virginia Water lake 300 metres north-west of McDougall's line at the junction of the London Road with Christchurch Road, and instead meets the London Road at SU 989696.

Part of the problem (as we saw in Chapter 3, Figure 13) lies with the location of Bakeham House, which was replaced by a house with the same name in the middle of the nineteenth century. Codrington said that Bakeham House was now called Upper Bakeham House. On the first Ordnance Survey six-inch plan about 1870, Upper Bakeham House stood near the present Alderhurst, 300 metres south of the later Bakeham House, and closer to the brow of the hill above Egham where in 1836 remains of Roman buildings and pottery were found (Plate 26). McDougall's line reaches the brow of the hill near Upper (old) Bakeham House, whereas Margary 4a, which projects the alignment from Duke's Hill, goes through the later Bakeham House.

In 1981 I got a permit from the Crown Estate to look in the Belvedere and Clock Case Wood, and in Windsor Park, to see if I could find the remains described by the Sandhurst cadets. There are two nearly parallel rides through the Belvedere Woods, dating back to nineteenth-century maps, but they are aligned north-east from Shrub's Hill, passing 200 metres south-east of the Belvedere Fort, at an angle to Margary 4a. The southern one, Cedar Drive, is raised partly on and partly alongside a very large embankment, which is also accompanied by several hollow ways. Prior to 1748 this had been the route taken by the London Road (Figure 30), as it appears on Norden's Plan of Windsor Great and Little Parks in 1607.[28] Correspondingly, to the east of Virginia Water Lake, between Broad Ride and the London Road on Cut Hill, there is a similar massive bank accompanied by hollow ways. This seemed to fit the road described by the Sandhurst cadets, as well as earlier descriptions of the Devil's Highway being on a massive embankment (Plate 27).

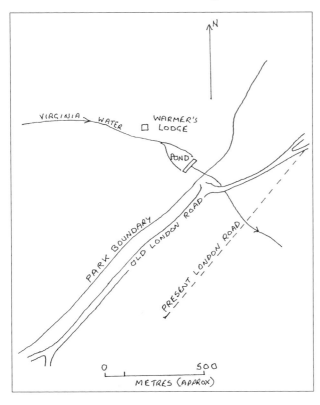

30 Tracing of the Old London Road from Norden's Map. This shows the main features on Norden's Map of 1607 which include the course of the Old London Road compared to its modern counterpart.

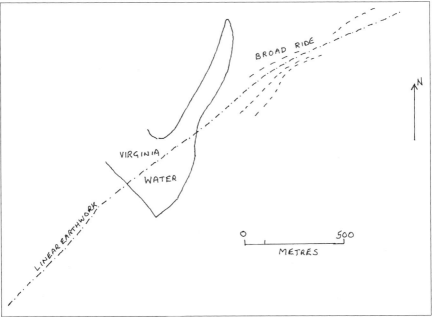

31 The linear earthwork crossing Virginia Water. This shows the route that appears to have been followed by the linear earthworks which traditionally formed the Devil's Highway, but was also the course of the old London Road.

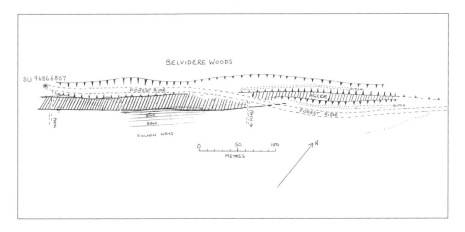

32 The linear earthwork in Belvedere Woods; a sketch made at the time, based on transect and offsets.

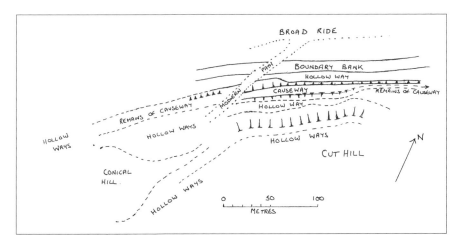

33 The ridges, including the linear earthwork south of Broad Ride, in Windsor Park. See also Plate 27.

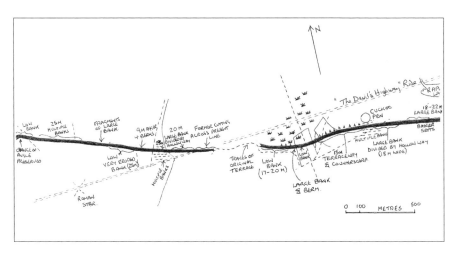

34 The linear earthwork between Easthampstead Plain and Cuckoo Pen near Rapley Lakes, with annotations indicating the nature and condition of the remains. Devil's Highway Ride is a post-medieval forest ride corresponding to Margary 4a.

However there was a flaw to this idea. Roman roads are (allegedly) invariably straight. The remains I had tracked down zigzagged, often significantly adrift of Margary 4a (see Figure 31). There was a change of direction in Sunningdale to cross Shrubs Hill. Then another change of direction 200 metres south-east of the Belvedere Fort to follow the forest ride south of Cedar Drive, with a third change of direction where Broad Ride meets the north-east arm of Virginia Water (Figure 31). Finally the earthwork met London Road pointing to Upper Bakeham House (that is the original Bakeham House). My linear earthwork only coincided with Margary 4a at two points, ironically one by the Roman columns on Blacknest Road. I found myself in the same situation I had encountered with Long Causeway five years before. I might have found some lengths of a large embankment, but they could not be the Roman road (Figures 32 and 33). I spent the next three years trying to prove the point, but to no avail. Even the fact that Margary 4a differs from McDougall's alignment, which in turn differs from the 1836 RMC description had no effect on the established view. There may be some interesting earthworks in the vicinity of Devil's Highway, but Devil's Highway is unquestionably Margary 4a.

There were similar differences between the alignment of the earthwork and Margary 4a either side of Rapley Lakes, near Bagshot. Figure 34 is an annotated sketchplan of the linear earthwork in relation to Devil's Highway Ride, identified as the Roman road according to Margary 4a.

The annotations identify the condition and nature of the remains. Between the circular enclosure Cuckoo Pen and the ascent onto Easthampstead Plain to the west, the eighteenth-century forest ride goes over the top of a small conical hill and through a marsh. The linear earthwork follows a more practical route close

35 These three photographs, with accompanying diagrams, show the linear earthwork obliquely crossing a hollow way supposed to have been made by the Romans.

36 These three photographs show sections of the linear earthwork west of Cuckoo Pen.

to the contour, and is accompanied by hollow ways indicating the old London Road. These branch southwards near Easthampstead Plain towards Wishmoor Cross and Camberley where the old London Road joined the old Portsmouth Road.

Figure 35 shows three views of the hollow way by means of which the forest ride (Margary 4a) ascends onto Easthamstead Plain. However the linear earthwork crosses the forest ride here, and can be seen converging on the south side of the hollow way, and diverging north of the top of the hollow way. It is hard to imagine how or why someone would line up the linear earthwork in this way if the hollow way was there when it was constructed: it looks like it predates the hollow way. However, according to Margary 4a the Romans made the cutting. The first picture in Figure 35 is the view looking down the cutting, the other two looking up the cutting from the south-east, with margin sketches to assist interpretation. Figure 36 shows the nature of the remains immediately west of Cuckoo Pen. It isn't easy to photograph low profile remains under conifers or in any other heavily vegetated landscapes, which is why annotated sketch plans like Figure 34 provide an important record. The survey pole used here is only one metre long (already seen in Plates 4 and 5).

I don't think amateurs are any more prone to the pitfalls of tracing Roman roads than professionals. Local historians wanting to pursue Roman roads or any other alignment, feel free to go ahead and indulge. Don't be discouraged by the opinions of others, but at the same time take care to check the reliability of the evidence.

Chapter Eight

EXPLORING SUBURBIA

It is likely that many readers of this book will live in towns and cities, and probably within easy walking distance from countryside to explore. The author has always lived in built-up areas, and only occasionally these have provided ready access to open country. Mostly it has meant walking through several miles of suburbia, or catching a bus to the nearest open country; for others it may be that fieldwork territory is only a few minutes by car. All the same, not everyone's need for local history fieldwork is based on going somewhere else. Local history is usually where you live.

Equally, most urban readers will not live in town centres, where there might be medieval buildings or remnants of a medieval town plan, such as burgages and precincts. While some centres are being refurbished to attract residents, it is fairly likely most urban local historians live in suburbs. In any case the exploration of a planned medieval town or an early post-medieval centre depends much more on documentary research than fieldwork. The subject matter of medieval towns is too big for a small chapter in a book on fieldwork. So what this chapter is really about is what you can do in suburbia.

Admittedly there are some areas of suburbia that are just row upon row of houses, with small gardens if any, and little means of envisaging how the landscape looked before. However there are also suburbs with open spaces, including parks and playing fields, linear corridors such as lanes, plantation strips, small stream courses and larger river banks. There are sometimes spaces between rows of houses, that were intended as allotments, or were not suited to building, either because of gradient, or the remains of quarrying or mining, or because they were not readily accessible. There are utilised open spaces such as golf courses, games pitches, and cemeteries which may still have evidence of the past. There are varying sizes of common land, which if not converted as public parks, are left as overgrown spaces. For the local historian these forgotten spaces are a bit daunting, and seem unlikely places to look for the past. They are often places you freely explored as a child, but no way would you go there an adult, unless you are one of the more intrepid dog-walkers. Yet they are much-neglected windows on the past.

The other dimension of suburbia is the configuration of the landscape before it was built over. Each area of housing was built in a plot of acquired land, some of the boundaries of which once divided fields, others divided medieval estates. Some of the roads perpetuate ancient roads. It is very easy to forget that much of suburbia, only a few decades ago, was open countryside, farmland, woodland and a few scattered cottages. The fact that houses have been superimposed on the landscape is only an obstacle to exploration; it doesn't take away the historic past, though it may destroy some of the physical remains. Some of the past in the landscape is still there beneath gardens, or a thread of the past interlinked across many gardens. So in suburbia, local history on the ground is not as unrealistic as it might first appear.

Although suburbs developed outside the gates of medieval towns, the phenomenon as we know it is a product of the late nineteenth and twentieth century. Before the mid-nineteenth century it was difficult to sell off parts of estates, as the estates had a fixed taxation value. So the first land to be developed outside towns was common land, and in W.G. Hoskins' pioneering work *The Making of the English Landscape* he describes how towns like Nottingham and Coventry eventually broke free of medieval overcrowding by converting Lammas lands into real estate, by overturning the constraints over their use by Acts of Parliament.[1] Other opportunities to develop land occurred where there were long established small land units such as church lands, and lands dedicated to charities or funding educational institutions, where the funding element could be converted to bonds or gilts and the land released for building. Changes to heritable jurisdictions and other commitments to keep estates intact, combined with the increasing financial burdens faced by the landed gentry, led to bits of estates being released for building. All these factors tended to produce a patchwork of small housing developments around towns, wherever opportunity allowed, rather than continuous outward growth.

So what we see today evolved through gradual infill of the spaces in between. As urban expansion accelerated, neighbouring parishes were absorbed, by the simple mechanism that towns could provide gas, reliable water supplies and other services, where communities on the rural fringes still depended on oil lamps and unreliable and often unhealthy wells. This absorption was inevitable but deferrable, as some parishes resisted the advances of neighbouring towns for decades, and again this piecemeal process has contributed to the patchwork evolution of suburbia. Both London and Birmingham, together with Glasgow, manifest the effects of this land hunger. There is a classic text by H.J. Dyos on the Victorian suburb of Camberwell in south London, which explores the evolutionary steps in the development of a suburb.[2]

The effect of this process is that boundaries of estates and parts of estates often survive in the suburban fabric, and different periods and styles of building distinguish one estate from another. The author's exploration of suburban Glasgow includes the graphic contrast between Cochrane's Lee and Maidlee (see Chapters One and Three), the former dominated by detached bungalows, the latter on rising ground, a dense jungle of gaunt terraces, the two juxtaposed across their medieval boundary. Thus, where you might think that tangible history is lost under the mass of suburbia, it is often relatively easy, with a bit of analysis of old and modern maps, and a bit of walking around, to recover a detailed picture of both the past landscape and the process that transformed it from rural idyll to urban sprawl.

Local history in the park

This leaves parks and commons. Parks are a good place to start. Some towns and cities were fortunate, usually in the late nineteenth or early twentieth century, to be given a park by landed gentry who could no longer afford the upkeep of a rambling mansion and even more rambling parkland. Others were able to buy the property, sometimes at a reasonable price, sometimes for an embarrassing fortune, with the commendable and honourable intention of making a tumbledown house into an emblem of civic pride. Invariably the intention depended on finding the considerably larger sums required to make good the leaking roofs and the woodworm-riddled timbers. There are some excellent examples around the country of majestic restorations, and a good many more that are burdensome liabilities, providing little income from a succession of lets, and often an abandoned shell. However, what also came with the house was some, or all, of the park, and usually, that park now serves for public leisure and recreation. What tends to be forgotten is that the setting for the big house is sometimes a historic setting. Admittedly some mansions were eighteenth or nineteenth century creations on farmland, built by wealthy merchants or industrialists. Others are in more or less the same position as the residences of medieval landowners and a few of them not too great a distance from the seats of their Saxon or Celtic counterparts, and some are even near a focal point for earlier settlers. Some parks are a window on the past.

However parks are not easy landscapes to explore. For one thing they contain successive fads for ornamentation and access. The private owners levelled lawns, excavated terraces, dug out lakes and artificial waterways, graded driveways and removed obstacles to desirable vistas, all with the purpose of leisure and impressing their visitors. They may have entirely reworked this landscape several times over to conform to a succession of fashions. The public owners can be just as destructive in creating the normal expectations of public leisure: sunken gardens and ponds, bowling greens and tennis courts, car parks and utilities. So the history on the ground may be very fragmented.

The other problem with public amenity is that where you walk is determined by tree and shrub-lined paths, where you may have to keep off the grass, and you certainly will not be popular with other users of the park if you emerge suddenly beside them from a shrubbery, or they sense you fighting through the undergrowth within inches of where they are sitting. Also parks are used by a variety of little understood sub-cultures, where people wander around certain areas looking for like-minded souls. So public parks are places where you need permission, and a good relationship with grounds staff, and may have to do your fieldwork at quiet times of day. The public are very defensive of their parks. Twice I have been accosted at length by concerned individuals totally convinced that I am secretly measuring up the park for a new supermarket. Dog walkers and canoodling couples do not understand anyone without a dog exploring woodland. However, if you can make practical arrangements to explore, parks can be very rewarding places to look for history on the ground.

Other parks are created out of former industrial land, either water-powered industry along river banks, or extractive industry where the quarry pits and hollows have been backfilled. Sometimes such landscapes are too greatly disturbed to be of much interest, but particularly those along river banks, or where there is land besides the disturbed component, can be rewarding to explore. Parks on formerly cultivated land have the same problems as rural cultivated land, but bear the advantage that they may have been imparked before deep ploughing altered the configuration of the landscape. Woodland parks make it difficult to visualise the shape of the underlying landscape, and difficult to follow linear features, or to keep a clear sense of location and direction. Some public parks are created out of common land, where the medieval uses were more transient, but there may be prehistoric archaeology. The important point to make, however, is that people often see public parks as modern landscapes, when in reality they are often valuable opportunities to explore over a much longer timescale. However, whereas in the countryside you need to keep right with the farmer, in parks you have to respect everybody else, and that can be quite difficult if there are people lying on the grass or playing football where you want to explore, or you encounter those sorts of dog owners whose dogs apparently have more rights than you and apparently every right to be suspicious of your intentions and to bark or bite. Dogs don't seem to understand humans who are similarly preoccupied with close inspection of the ground, and your own dog may be of the same persuasion.

Other open spaces

Another kind of suburban open space is recreation-specific: football or rugby pitches, dug into and built out of slopes, running tracks, and golf courses. Golf courses create a very striking landscape which from the air looks like snail-trails: linear fairways alternating with woodland, scrub and grass wilderness. Although golf course landscaping creates artificial mounds and hollows, it often preserves the previous landscape in between, including the corrugations of ridge-and-furrow landscapes, and the courses of old boundary banks and routeways. There may be the remains of earthworks or the foundations of past settlements neatly merged into the artificial landscape of the course. There is just one problem: access. Even if you can get permission, at your own risk, you have to be continually observant for the direction of play, as even in the rough there is a risk of injury from high velocity projectiles. Some golf courses may let you on in the early morning, but as some golfers are out as early as 7am that may mean fieldwork at 5am. Many golf courses, wary of insurance liability, may not let you on at all. Playing fields sometimes have quite interesting low profile surface remains, but the introduction of levelling and re-grading machinery in recent years has meant a rapid disappearance of such evidence.

One of the dangers of fieldwork in suburban open spaces is the proliferation of culverts, ducts and cable routes. On the present surface these may present no more

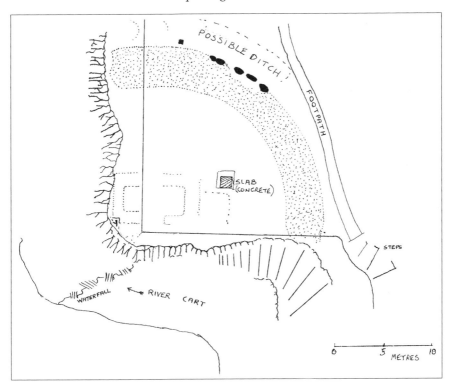

37 Busby Glen fort near Glasgow: relabelled pencil sketch made in 1970. See also Plate 28.

than a low rise or furrow, but sometimes appear as a more marked earthwork, especially if there are no manhole covers or vents as clues. In parks, the sites of tennis courts or swings and roundabouts can leave puzzling patterns, so it is wise to check large-scale Ordnance Survey map editions covering several decades, and always useful to keep on good terms with ground staff. As a student I spent my summers as a parks department groundsman. This gave rise to an amusing conflict of interest as the district clerk who authorised my wage packet was the local historian of the day, and my watchful presence on what he regarded as his patch was carefully monitored. However it enabled me to learn about both the pitfalls and the possibilities, including a certain mineshaft that looked like a prehistoric house platform (see Chapter One). Several of the parks I worked included former landfill, which helped me learn to distinguish recent from ancient surfaces. However they also gave access to river banks and areas of wasteland, which I would explore in my own time, having established the best ways in and out.

One of the parks near where I grew up was Busby Glen, which was a small riverside park that had been gifted by a mill owner around 1900. The remains of the cotton mills were on the left bank of the White Cart Water, the park on the right, above and beyond the weir atop a natural waterfall, from which the head of water for two mills had been drawn, the lower mill by means of a tunnel. The park is a narrow strip of land between the ravine below the waterfall and the railway embankment approaching a viaduct. Most of the space is a steep slope, but with a small area of grass for a children's play area. Yet within this small park I made several unexpected finds that inspired my fieldwork for decades after. The first, when I was twenty, was a promontory fort, formed in an angle of the ravine by a curved rampart, containing nearly a quarter of a circle with an internal radius of 17 metres.[3] The bank was four metres thick with large earth-fast rocks forming its outwards face (Figure 37 & Plate 28). The second find, two years later, was the remains of a mill, partly buried by rockfalls, on a ledge above the river within the ravine. I later found that the mill was well documented back to 1489.[4] In Chapter One, I described how then a decade later, in another small park, I found medieval pottery in the roots of a fallen tree, which revealed the location of a castle which I was subsequently able to research from documents. By that time, however, I was a committed and enthusiastic explorer of urban parks.

Parks around existing antiquities

Just as many parks have developed around a mansion house due to a gift of such land or an opportune purchase, some parks have been developed around significant antiquities, such as standing castles or the earthworks and foundations of castles. Far from discouraging exploration, on the grounds the evidence at the site is already known, having a key monument within a park should be added encouragement to look closer. Ancient monuments did not exist in isolation in the past, even if we isolate them today, and there would have been dependent buildings and enclosures around them, defensive outworks, routeways and utilities filling the whole space of the park and beyond. Not all evidence will be obvious, and often it will have been confused and fragmented by later landscaping, so that finding out will test all your skills of observational detective work. It is possible, for example, that known earthworks in parks will not be as accurately recorded as you might expect, and sometimes the interpretation of such remains is quite bizarre. This extends to earthworks anywhere: the main recorded features may not be the whole picture, and it is a useful exercise, in any case, to try to map peripheral features for practice in observation (see examples in the next chapter).

An illustration of peripheral earthworks occurs at Earl's Barton in Northamptonshire. Bury Hill is an enigmatic mound next to the church, which is defended by a wide and deep ditch in an arc on the north side. North of this, before recent landscaping, there were traces of an enclosure extending out from the ditch, J/G1 to E on the east side, and H through A2 to A on the west (Figure 38). At the north-west corner are some further foundations and ditches. However the low relief of these annexes, much altered by later landscaping, bears no comparison with the scale of Bury Hill earthwork, giving rise to some sceptical reactions to the additional remains.

The truth is that most earthwork remains – in the absence of conclusive documentary evidence – are subject to interpretation. Thus several people can interpret the remains in entirely different ways. This apparent frailty is one of the key arguments archaeologists use to justify systematic fieldwork (walking in

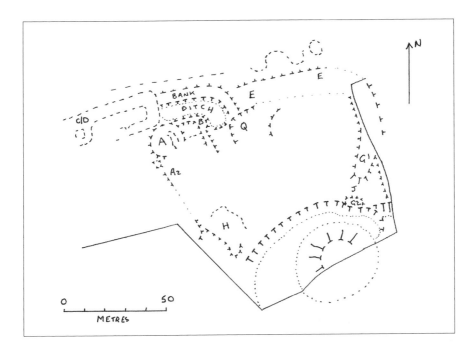

38 Bury Hill, Earls Barton showing remains north of the ditch. It is always worth looking at the environs of known monuments, especially in public parks. The low profile remains of an enclosure can be seen north of the ditch, formed by features G2/J/G1 curving round as E, through a complex of features around Q, B, A and A2, before returning at H.

parallel lines noting features). Their approaches are supposed to eliminate these inconsistencies between interpreters. But the same interpretation issues affect other disciplines such as ecology and geology, and their practitioners aren't forced to walk dispassionately in parallel lines. Rather, an interpretative approach affords the local historian some opportunity to contribute to the discussion by means of fieldwork, to add fresh insight into what might be there.

There is a very good illustration of a debateable earthwork in a park on the south side of Glasgow. Queen's Park is landscaped around the slopes of a prominent hill, known as Camp Hill, on top of which there is supposed to have been an ancient fortification. The last person to describe it so was Hugh MacDonald in 1854, who wrote that it was the 'vestiges of an ancient British camp' and that 'it occupied the entire crown of the eminence, and was upwards of a hundred yards in diameter.'[5] In the 1860s the owner carried out extensive excavations of the site, digging as far down as eight feet, but no record survives of what was found; he apparently created an enclosed plantation on the site. The mystery is that since the late nineteenth century this camp seems to have slipped off the top of the hill, and now only skirts the western edge, with most of the enclosure on a slope, and very little level ground within. The summit is now mostly occupied by a flagpole mount and paved or tarmac paths which allow access to different vantage points

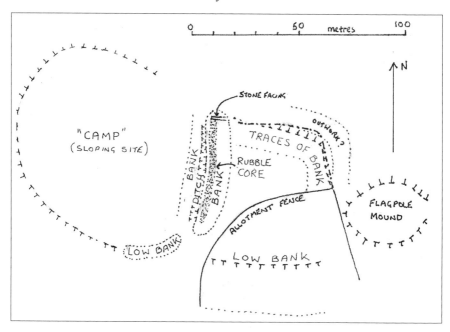

39 Camp Hill, Queen's Park, Glasgow. McDonald described it as on the summit in 1854, however in more recent times it has been argued that the camp is a nineteenth-century plantation boundary on the steep slopes to the west; 'Camp' on plan.

and seating areas from which to take in the view from the hill. Understanding of the site nowadays hinges on the surviving rampart on the western crest of the hill (Figure 39), which has a rubble core (stippled on plan), and a small ditch and bank west. Stone facings at the northern end suggest that the defences turned east, along the north edge of the summit, and then south to form a rectangle on the hilltop. However its southern end appears to continue south-west to become the circuit on the hillside ('Camp'). Which is the fort, the top of the hill or the enclosure on the western slopes?

Sometimes just one small observation can make all the difference. Castledykes Park in Dumfries, besides a garden in the floor of an old quarry, is almost entirely made up of two castle earthworks: Castledykes and Paradise. The conventional interpretation is that Paradise, which consists of a rocky knoll as the motte (D on Figure 40), and a level platform as the bailey (E, F, G), is the earlier castle, while Castledykes to the east is a much larger enclosure used by both the Scots and the English during the first of the Scottish Wars of Independence at the end of the thirteenth and the beginning of the fourteenth century.[6] It was Castledykes that Edward I of England was bound for when he died at Grange over Sands on 7 July 1307; records show in the preceding days his forces had been stocking it with supplies for his arrival.[7] The odd thing about these two castle earthworks is that they are only 40 metres apart, and it is hard to imagine that the Paradise earthworks were excluded from Castledykes, when they could readily be seized by a besieging enemy, especially as they are closer to the River Nith, where supplies

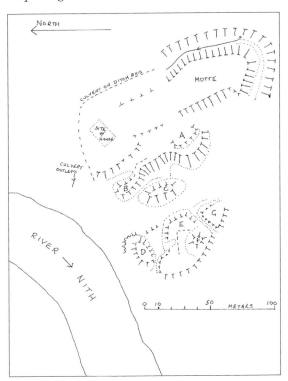

40 Castle Dykes, Dumfries. The feature known as 'The Saddle' is identified as C on the plan. The Paradise motte is at D, E, F, and G, forming a D-shape. The main motte to the east has outworks at A and B which are indented to accommodate C. Yet no previous accounts of the castles ever mention The Saddle at C. Even known monuments in public parks deserve scrutiny.

could be landed. Visiting Castledykes Park at the 700th anniversary of Edward's death, the writer noticed that a mound known as The Saddle on old plans (C), was exactly midway between the two, and co-aligned between a projection of the bailey of Paradise motte at E, and an inturn in the bailey of Castledykes (between A and B). In fact, the presence of just one, previously unnoticed mound, The Saddle, proves that both formed one castle, a triangle with sides of about 130 to 140 metres. Perhaps as a result of modifications to improve the defences, or as a result of Robert de Bruce demolishing the defences, the two 'castles' had come to be seen as independent features.

A third example of multiplicity of interpretations occurs at Abington Park in Northampton, already visited in Chapters Four and Five. Gifted to Northampton by Lady Wantage in 1895,[8] the park is based on the landscaped surrounds of the manor house; a further area was later purchased from the estate.[9] There are fish ponds, several enlarged as modern ponds, and one converted to a sunken rose garden. More importantly there are the streets and surviving foundations of a village displaced to a new location half a mile south at the end of the seventeenth century, during improvements to the park. A plan survives from 1671, before the village was moved, and another from the eighteenth century.[10] The modern park also preserves good examples of ridge-and-furrow, including alternating ridge and grass strips, together with the medieval road eastwards from Northampton through Weston Favell to Wellingborough, and a variety of unexplained earthworks. The debateable element is part of the northbound street in the

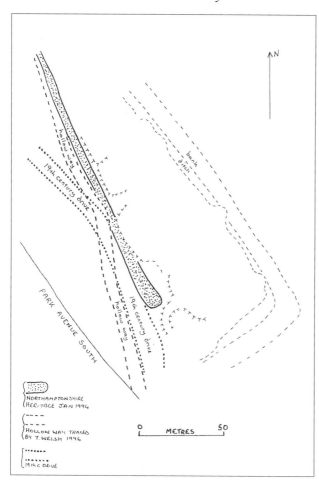

41 Abington Park overlying routes. This is a simplification of Figure 19. The hollow way is shown by a broken line and the nineteenth-century drive which crosses it by a dotted line. When re-examined by archaeologists in 1995, they interpreted the medieval street (stippled) east of the nineteenth-century drive. Classic 'stratigraphy'.

former village. When the Royal Commission produced a plan of the village in 1985 they showed ridge and furrow extending right up to the street from the east,[11] however this extended across the visible foundations of houses. When the local archaeology unit revised the plan in 1995, they depicted these houses.[12] But they introduced an improbable angular change in direction in the north street which doesn't appear on the 1671 plan.

What had happened at Abington Park was that the original driveway from the north lodge (Archway Cottages) followed the line of the north street. In the mid-nineteenth century a new entrance drive was created from a gate 200 metres south-west (Figure 41). This curved across the line of the north street, and was constructed over the foundations of three houses on the east side of the older street, before curving south-west towards the mansion house (Figure 19 also shows this arrangement). It was tree lined. The true course of the north street lies under the curve of the nineteenth-century drive, which crosses it twice as a raised causeway, and house foundations on the west side of the old street can still be seen within the curve of the modern drive. This is classic 'stratigraphy'. The 1995 plan mistook the dip east of the curve of the nineteenth-century drive for the continuation of the hollow way, even though this ran behind the houses on the east side of the 1671 street (refer back to Figure 19). There is always potential to add to knowledge by re-interpreting or re-evaluating the official record of what is there, even if the remains are low in profile and not very photogenic.

While some mansion houses became the focal points of public parks, others remain in private hands, whether as private residences, or as company headquarters, clinics, schools and colleges or other institutional buildings. The grounds therefore may be just as productive, in terms of local history on the ground, as similarly derived public parks; they just involve a different process for gaining permission to take a look. The University of Northampton's Park Campus, where the author has been based for sixteen years, is on the site of an Elizabethan mansion, built within the circuit of a medieval deer park. Part of the deer park boundary, together with the site of the mansion, and a ha-ha can be seen in close proximity in a planted green space amidst the university buildings.

Commons

Some parks are based on commons, either as formalised parks or as semi-wild environments. Legislation allowed many commons to be converted into public parks.[13] Also, where commons were unavoidably encroached by railways, roads, or essential housing, another piece of waste land was given in compensation, so that many urban commons end up as an admix of unwanted pieces of land. Their value to local history on the ground depends on the history of their usage. Sometimes this is recorded in local histories, or may be held by the local church or the local authority if there were minutes and records of commons trustees. Some commons were used for grazing livestock and/or haymaking. Others were used as a source of raw materials, including cutting peat, digging sand and gravel, or collecting firewood. After about 1880 many commons were converted to Poor's Allotments to provide an income to pay for winter fuel or to help maintain almshouses. Some of these were given over to forestry, as a source of revenue, or leased for other uses such as golf courses. So in some cases the land surface has been greatly altered by peat diggings, gravel and sand pits. However, some commons are based on land that in prehistoric times was valued as a place of defence or for burial, so although medieval remains may be lacking, commons may contain valuable clues about earlier times. Large commons often had to be crossed by lines of communication, so the remains of old roads may survive where they wouldn't have been preserved on farmland.

Figure 42 shows a turf-cut enclosure on Thurstaston Common in the Wirral, which demonstrates some of the problems of 'stratification' encountered in Chapter Four, although most of the disturbances are recent. The top diagram shows the main features, while the lower diagram explains the sequences. Apart from modern paths criss-crossing the site there is an old boundary bank and ditch, ridge-and-furrow and modern drains to consider. An old field boundary crossing south-west to north-east appears to pass under the enclosure at A, but

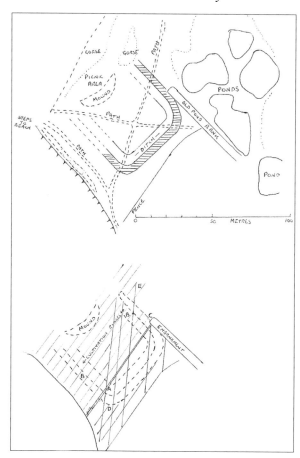

42 Thurstaston Common, Wirral. This is an essay in 'stratigraphy' although the overlying features are mostly recent. The upper diagram shows the main features, and the lower shows how the remains relate to cultivation ridges, boundary banks and drainage ditches.
Relationships:
A: Boundary not evident in bank & ditch
B: Cultivation ridges have reduced evidence of bank
C: Pond bank overlaps earthwork
D: Drains not seen on bank
E Cultivation ridges extend beyond bank.

over it towards the embankment ending at C. The cultivation ridges parallel to this appear mostly later, but do not show in part of the ditch at B. The embankment for the ponds appears to overlap part of the enclosure at C. Some apparent drains pass under the earthwork, whilst others running north and south clearly overlie it.

Figure 43 shows an additional ditched enclosure near the north-east corner of a recorded medieval moat in a public open space along a footpath right-of-way in Preston, examined in 1991. The location is Broughton, in the north-east corner of built-up Preston, near Sharoe Green. The moat, which uses the stream as its north side, is nowadays much neglected. The additional earthworks lie on the north bank of the stream in what was long grass and scrub at the time, and suggest there was an additional moated area containing several building platforms (1 and 2). However there is a concrete structure (S) in the moat which warns of the possibility of more recent explanation. A pond and other remains were also noted. The importance of including this is that, whatever the explanation for the features, often peripheral evidence around known sites goes unrecorded. The potential local history interest may have been missed.

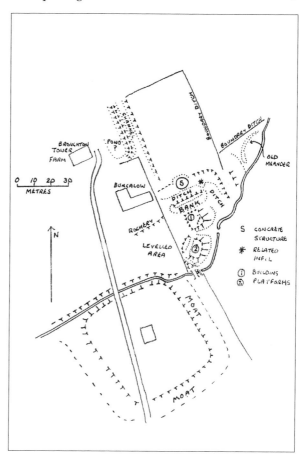

43 Earthworks adjoining Broughton Moat, Preston. These lie north-east of the known moat on the north bank of the stream.

Riverside parks and open access along riversides also forms an important resource for local history on the ground. So much of past human life focussed upon rivers, for food supply, water-power and travel, and were also barriers to communication where it was necessary to find safe crossing points, and adjuncts to defence. Cultivation until modern times did not extend up to the banks or the crests of valleys, as the woodland and scrubland had other uses as a cover for game or a source of materials, so earthworks, building remains and other evidence of the past have a good chance of survival. In 1837 the Wellingborough historian John Cole described a barrow on the banks of Swanspool Brook:[14]

In the meadows on the verge of Swan's-pool rivulet, about half a mile from Croyland Hall, is a mound, much resembling one of those everlasting sepulchres of the ancients called tumuli. This tumulus, if so we may be allowed to designate it, is not more than three or four feet high, but its circumference, measuring round the ditch which encloses it, is about one hundred yards.

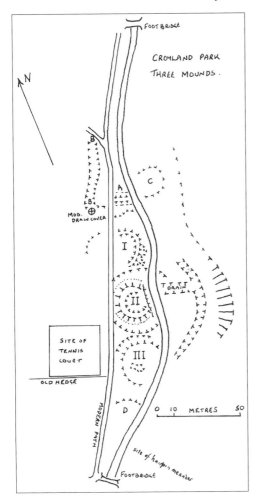

44 Cole's Barrow, Croyland Park, Wellingborough. These three mounds survive in a playing field between a footpath and the Swanspool Brook; II is the mound described by Cole, I and III are lesser mounds; other features in the vicinity denoted A–D.

The mound, with its surrounding ditch about 33 metres in diameter, and parts of two circular features north and south of it, survive to this day, although they were not rediscovered until 2001 (II on Figure 44). The streamside lies in a modern park, with football pitches, and a former tennis court is very close to the mound. Cultivation until recent times had not encroached the mound, which still has a ditch around it, and is undercut by the stream, just as Cole described displaced stones: 'It would appear that, through the continued underminings of the brook, they had been washed from the encompassing fosse, which is broken into in this part.' Although the stream is itself capable of removing the remains, given time, proximity to the stream has been the reason that the barrow has survived for so long. So that even in a suburban environment an open space can preserve as much history on the ground as its rural counterpart.

Suburbs may not appear to be good locations for finding local history on the ground, but a closer inspection of open spaces may provide much more information than expected.

Chapter Nine

EXPLORING VILLAGES

On the other hand there will be local historians engaging with rural parishes and villages. I think we have got into a mindset, with landscape history often directed at parish and village landscapes, that we know all there is to know about villages. So for local historians in villages I anticipate there must be a real anxiety about adding to local knowledge through fieldwork. After all there's surely not much to add to the basic components of church, village green, maybe nominal castle hill or moat, and the mill? To the writer, villages are fun to explore, because there's a real challenge to find evidence that contradicts that simplicity. I personally feel a strong urge to defy the rules, break down barriers, and turn everything upside down.

There is also an anachronism here. Exploring suburbs involves, to a large extent, exploring villages absorbed into urban jungles. The difference is not just that there's more visible green space. The manor and its surrounding parkland are probably still private rather than public. Rather than a lord of the manor it is probably now owned or leased by an institution or a company headquarters, and not that easy to access. Woodland may be where a farmer rears his pheasants, and riverside walks may be carefully regulated by angling club arrangements with farmers. Villages are usually surrounded by working farmland, so all those fields may be under crop or grazed by animals the farmer doesn't want disturbed or harmed by walkers intent on counterproductive pursuits like history. Some farmers seem mortally afraid of someone finding something that needs to be preserved and hence restricts their freedom. Also, in many villages there seems to be an informal licence to walk the dog around a succession of fields, but the moment you go there without a dog, head down, puzzling over banks and hollows it is suddenly suspicious behaviour. So ironically there is often less freedom to roam in potentially useful landscapes in a village than in a suburb.

Right through this book, I can only re-iterate that archaeology and local history have gone their separate ways, and landscape history seems to have followed the archaeology lead. There seem to have been changes in the way we approach landscapes over the past thirty years that have somehow taken the fun out of local history on the ground. Where villages are concerned, there was a change of perspective in the 1970s, where archaeology borrowed from social geography, in order to simplify and classify villages. Although this writer has an interest in historical geography, the passion some people have for theoretical models of how villages evolved has never found any appeal. Readers must make up their own minds about this. I don't think there is any doubt that most villages can be likened to one model or another, but I personally feel the models are too prescriptive. Villages shouldn't be 'failures' because they don't fit the models for an ideal classification, and indeed the villages that don't fit might be all the more interesting, were the models that crucial to understanding them.

My perception of local historians is that they want to find out about where they live, not whether their village or town meets certain national criteria, so at risk of conflict with the pro-model lobby I'm going to be iconoclastic here. This writer is passionate about exploring villages, but just exploring and finding out; inquisitive but not concerned about classification. That may not suit all my readers, but at least you now know where I'm coming from. Each village is the sum of all the people who lived and worked in it over the centuries. Some villages owe more to the influence of power holders, such as the lord of the manor (especially in 'closed' villages); others to strong influences within the community (usually 'open' villages). So we should look at each village on its own merits.

The classic text on exploring villages was written by Joscelyne Finberg in 1958, which explores every detail of village layouts, building plans, building construction and evidences of manorial power in the landscape.[1] You might look at the plan, but only to determine if the village had shrunk, or how it was composed around the church or the green, or in relation to landscape considerations such as shelter. The operating principle was observation and interpretation; an ideal approach for the local historian. W.G. Hoskins, in *The Midland Peasant* looked at one Leicestershire village, Wigston Magna, in 1965, and explored in depth through both documents and fieldwork, how the village related to its forebears and to the various forces that impinged on it, such as the manor.[2] The last inquisitive approach to villages was in *Landscape Archaeology* by Aston and Rowley in 1974.[3] In their Chapter Six, on fieldwork in villages, they pose questions, such as 'why does this road turn at right-angles to the rectory garden?' (p118). They look at the village plan, but warn that 'any attempt to classify village plans is fraught with difficulties' (p121). They look at the road pattern, the land parcels, the green and the church. It is the kind of village exploration that suits me, and perhaps most readers will feel the same way.

Only four years later, in 1978, Trevor Rowley's book *Villages in the Landscape* appeared.[4] In this the analysis of village plans is far more detailed, looking at the processes of change. Rowley expresses the need for the fieldworker to examine the site 'from the point of view of geology, soils, communications and the availability of water', something that persists in archaeology texts as we saw in Chapter Six. His book remains a first-rate guide to understanding villages, but it introduces the spectre of theoretical modelling, drawing on Michael Chisholm's 1968 study of rural settlements: relating the village to the resources exploited. Rowley reproduces Chisholm's village location diagram, giving different weightings to arable and grazing land, building materials, water and fuel. The inquisitive approach is losing out to the theoretical and classification-based approach that is deemed essential for archaeology. By the time of Aston's *Interpreting the Landscape* in 1985, modelling and classification are much more prominent.[5] However for the local historian, trying to understand the documentary evidence with reference to the landscape, and looking for documentary evidence to account for discoveries made through fieldwork, the driving force is more inquisitive and exploratory in nature. It isn't about whether the village adheres to established rules or fits the standard model. It is a quest for explanation that is both historical and drawn from observations.

The inquisitive approach to villages

In this book I have advocated what I have termed an 'inquisitive' strategy: a strategy for exploring the landscape in order to find out how it serves or impedes human activity, in the past and in the present. I have used the term 'inquisitive' to offset the more prescriptive approaches advocated by archaeologists (recognising some archaeologists believe their prescriptive survey methods to be inquisitive enough). The local historian can achieve this by asking questions about the landscape, with reference to some basic frameworks offered as a guide. In part this thinking owes some debt to the Aston and Rowley format: 'why does this road turn at right angles to the rectory garden?' However it is also about how we move through the landscape to ask such questions. Where local history differs from archaeology, in this context, is that local historians want to understand their own landscape better, whereas archaeologists seek to control information with a view to classification and inventory, and shun subjective 'following your nose' approaches. It is important to have some sort of strategy for exploration, but it should be one that explores what the landscape has to offer, and learns from the landscape. Strategies that superimpose systematic ways of surveying may help archaeologists, but they do not benefit local historians.

It is also important to be aware of the landscape, which in an environment covered by houses, outbuildings, tarmac roads, high privacy walls and not always readily accessible woods is not always that approchable. So it is vital to establish a link with the underlying landscape. To give an example of this thinking, you could look round the present village from within, asking questions about present-day configurations: 'why does this road turn?' Or you could approach the village from outside, or from high vantage points, or follow different roads or lanes through and around. You need fresh perspectives, in order to be able to ask those questions about how people might have lived in, worked with and moved across the surrounding landscape, and how that might have affected the evolution of the village.

In short, the answer, in this author's view, is to turn the whole thing upside down. Forget about theories as to why the village conforms to a given layout. Let's really get to grips with what the landscape did for the village, and still does. To do that you need to get away from the confines of present village layout – like why the main street is long and wide, or why this road turns – and find fresh perspectives. Modern street scenes often hide older patterns, especially if the road network has changed from its medieval counterpart, either through eighteenth-century planned village developments, or nineteenth-century re-alignment to turnpike roads or railways. These perspectives include looking at the shapes and sizes of spaces, using vantage points to study different facets of the village, and looking at barriers such as watercourses as well as the potential benefits of water courses. Only once you have 'unravelled' the village by turning your attention to the landscape on which it evolved can you really begin to explore village history on the ground.

Exploring space

The first of these ideas lies with spaces. We tend to think of spaces as wide streets or village greens or other communal places like playing fields or the churchyard. However spaces can be in terms of building plot shapes and sizes, such as tofts or other compositional land units, together with the non-standard spaces in between them. They could be simply the spaces between the existing road network, without regard to artificial boundaries within, or the way blocks and divisions are arranged around the topography. They include the shapes and sizes of individual fields, and any evidence of the pre-enclosure pattern of rigs and furlongs. So the spaces can be within the village and adjacent to it and can include up to a kilometre radius around the village if need be. There are a number of questions to be asked here: what might have determined particular shapes and sizes, or what are the influencing factors? It could also include why some spaces have houses in them and others are pasture, or scrub woodland. The spaces can be empty or filled.

This is an important task in many villages, with the pressure to fill every available space with affordable homes as well as homes for well-heeled commuters once the traditional housing stock has been taken over. In many villages, sometimes only within the last decade, every usable space has been filled. Because of the need for orchards, horticulture, small arable plots and stock enclosures, many villages had a pattern of small irregular plots close to the houses and outbuildings that formed the village proper. Also where villages had shrunk due to the abandonment of house plots, further small spaces were created, difficult to cultivate because of earthworks and building remains. Nowadays these are more easily amalgamated into large field arable, or acquired as building plots for new homes. Until comparatively recent times they were utilised as paddocks for grazing animals. Even within small-holding plots in a village the outlines of smaller plots may still be visible on the ground. Because of the pace at which these are being incorporated into cultivated land or built on, a valuable role for local historians is to record any surface remains within them, and research their history through documents and old maps and plans.

There are usually sound reasons for odd-shaped plots. On the edge of Brixworth village in Northamptonshire there was, until recent times, a triangular piece of land, the apex of which is now absorbed into the surrounding field, which appears on a sixteenth-century map as 'Hall Barns'. The plot of land contains incomplete earthworks including a circular feature, a ditched enclosure and building platforms. It is possible that it was left uncultivated because the remains were difficult to remove, but used instead for barns and outbuildings. The triangular shape simply best fitted round the earlier remains. Other odd-shaped plots may have been woodland at one time, or ground used to deposit stones cleared from fields that have themselves been moved elsewhere. If there is visible ridge and furrow in a small plot in one direction, or otherwise not co-aligned with adjacent ridge and furrow, could this be re-use of ground as cultivated land after it had ceased to serve a different purpose? Sometimes enclosures or moated sites or other functional land units, once obsolete, were turned over to strip cultivation that preserved something of the original outline. Small rectangular plots bounded by ditches might have been to enclose orchards, barns or gardens, but can also be 'defended' areas such as monastic granges (see below).

Prospects and vantage points

Another way of approaching fieldwork in and around villages is to make good use of any available vantage points. This might be achieved by following any footpaths and roads that allow you to view the village and its environs from different angles. It may be necessary to ask farmers if you can make use of high ground that is only accessible by crossing their fields. In flatter landscapes the church tower may be accessible, or if someone can speak up for you, convince the owners of any big houses with good views to let you have access to them. A convenient way to see the landscape is by bus, especially if it's a double-decker, and if there is an embanked railway line passing your area a train journey can also be useful. The landscape may pass by very quickly with trees getting in the way, and interrupted vision due to cuttings or buildings, but an amazing amount of landscape interpretation can be done from trains, if you can just work out where the features are on a map. It is also amazing what you can see from the top of a double-decker bus, especially if you can get the front seat, and other passengers do not get too worried by you following the route on a map, and frantically taking notes. It is surprising how concerned some people can be if you are reading a map on the bus, and some have this unstoppable desire to try to tell you where you are. The view from the top deck gets you above the hedge line, and allows a clear view of features in fields. It would be a productive venture for a local history society to hire a double-decker or an open-topped touring bus, just to explore in this way.

The writer has made a number of discoveries from trains and buses, and a good example of such chance discovery arose in December 1989, while the bus was held up by an accident, just before construction began on the Freckleton bypass, on the road from Lytham St Annes to Preston in Lancashire. Freckleton is a small village on an inlet of the Ribble estuary that once provided shelter for fishing boats, but is linked with its neighbour Warton by modern housing on the fringes of an airfield (where I worked at the time). At the point where there is now a roundabout, I noticed a small plot of land that had been an orchard. There appeared to be a shallow moat round it (Figure 45).

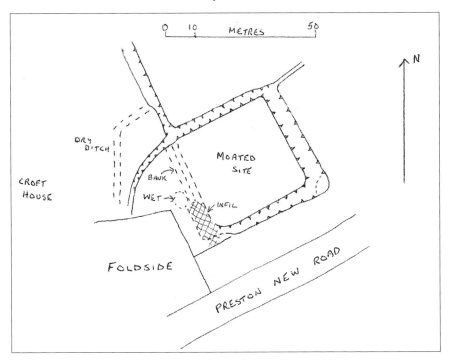

45 Freckleton Moat, near Preston. The original sketchplan shortly after discovery.

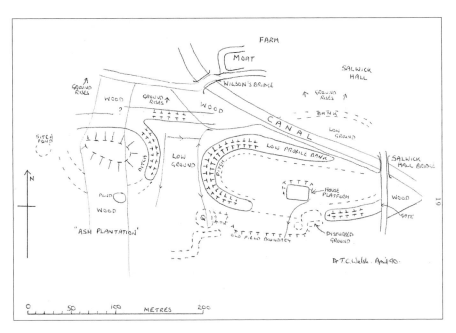

46 Salwick earthworks. This plan was previously published in *Archaeology North-West* No 4 Autumn/Winter 1992 p17.

At the earliest opportunity I got permission to visit the site, through a land agent, as the owner did not live locally. What I had seen from the bus was a rectangular plot 36 metres by 32 metres contained by a silted up moat five metres wide. This had possibly been for a monastic grange, as several are recorded for that parish. When it was excavated in advance of the roundabout no internal structures were found except for a cobbled surface on one side, but a large quantity of medieval pottery was found.[6] Several years later, in January 1993, I was interviewed on Radio Lancashire about how the discovery came to be made from the top deck of a bus. The archaeologist on the excavation and I were interviewed to draw attention to how the public could help record archaeological evidence, especially where threatened by development. This seemed the answer to my quest a decade earlier (see Chapter One) but in most of Britain local people are only invited to be involved in very restrictive ways, such as those so-called community archaeology projects where volunteers walk in parallel lines, and aren't permitted to think for themselves.

Not far from Freckleton, at Salwick, there are remains of an enclosure cut by the Lancaster Canal, and another to the west, which first came to my attention after frequently spotting them from a passing train. They lie south of the small medieval moat at Salwick Hall Farm, though not in an apparent village location now, being close to the atomic energy research centre (Figure 46). There are similarities to an enclosure at nearby Treales Village (Figure 47); this one was spotted after a liquid lunch, having crossed to road from the pub to look at the view through a gap in the hedge. I was just at the right location to see the enclosure to advantage, which proves the point that fresh vantage points, however unorthodox, pay dividends. It has long been suspected there might be an early enclosure at Treales, because the name, previously written Treweles or Treveles, has been suggested to derive from *tref* (a unit of land) and *lis* meaning a court or hall.[7] Figure 48 shows the named field units from the tithe award map revealing how this mysterious enclosure fitted into the landscape.

Looking at earthworks

Many villages have earthworks representing former houses, gardens, yards and roads, if the village has shrunk or re-aligned to new routways. These may appear on large-scale Ordnance Survey maps or in archaeological accounts of the area, such as a Royal Commission inventory. For many historians they are there to see, but not necessarily easy to explain, and it may be that it seems there is little more to be done. However, if you recall Chapter Four, in the second and subsequent steps for interpretation of remains, I wrote in rather a lot of detail about the need to look at relationships and interfaces between component earthworks. Local historians can add a great deal of knowledge about village earthworks by identifying overlaps and that dreaded term 'stratigraphy', as well as picking up subtler components that have been missed. Again, during the 1970s, there was a change in the way these were recorded and mapped. Originally they were painstakingly mapped out by ground survey. Air photo archaeology made it easier

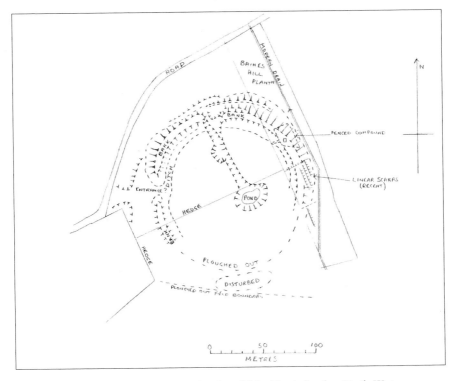

47 Treales earthwork. This plan was previously published in *Archaeology North-West*.

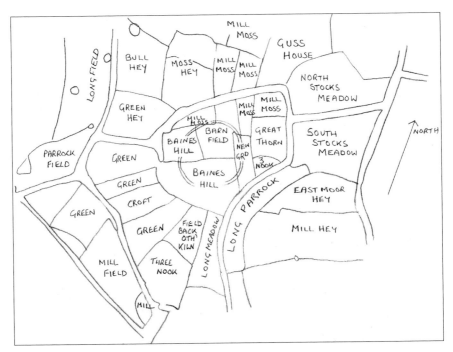

48 Treales tithe award field names showing fields radiating from the earthwork.

to spot such earthworks as well as to map them, so often what is recorded is what was obvious from air photographs. Only if the earthworks were unusual or significant was there any follow up by the increasingly expensive process of ground survey.

This change had unfortunate consequences. It is relatively easy to spot earthwork patterns from the air, along with crop marks and soil marks indicating buried archaeology lacking surface manifestation due to ploughing. However these may extend into adjacent woodland or scrub, or through less readily visible ground where there is shadow from buildings or a belt of trees, or just ground that doesn't favour aerial viewing. These aerially invisible remains have seldom been picked up since the 1970s. That would seem to suggest great opportunities for local historians, which was true probably into the 80s and maybe into the early 90s. However since the 1990s we have had housing infill, for supposedly affordable homes as well as rural homes for urban workers, new roads, and the amalgamation of small plots into larger fields, as explained above. Thus these opportunities are rapidly disappearing, and in many villages these unrecorded remains have already gone. The writer explored many villages in Northamptonshire from the mid-90s, barely able to keep up with redevelopment, and because this counts as local history rather than 'real archaeology' unable to do much to publish the evidence found. It is frustrating that air photo archaeology replaced on-the-ground fieldwork just at the worst possible time, when much of our rural heritage was being destroyed by needed development. With that constraint, a really worthy cause for local historians interested in local history on the ground is to record these uncharted earthworks before they all vanish.

Of course the remains that turn up in this way may not be that exciting archaeologically, as they are likely to include more abandoned medieval and post-medieval house platforms, evidence of pre-improvement farming activities, utility enclosures and linear earthworks of the more commonplace kind. However getting to understand these better is useful to the local historian, and only by searching through this material do you have a chance of making a breakthrough discovery, like part of a lost medieval moat, or medieval fish ponds, or remains of Iron Age settlement. Where crop marks have been reported close to a village, sometimes searches of adjacent woodland and pasture will reveal surface remains that relate to the crop marks. It is astonishing how often photographs of interesting crop marks are published when no-one has checked adjoining ground, or for that matter, checked old maps and plans for more recent explanations. Between Church Brampton and Chapel Brampton in Northamptonshire a classic group of prehistoric crop marks is actually based on a lane linking two farmhouses around pre-enclosure units, and the lane corresponds to opposing gateways between buildings either side of the farmyard at Brampton Hill. It is astonishing how many crop marks are classed as prehistoric, that could be demonstrated to be medieval or post-medieval by the dedicated efforts of local historians. Yet at Church Brampton, only 500 metres west, and next to the church, only a small proportion of earthworks is recorded in the Royal Commission Inventory,[8] that include fish ponds, a mill and house platforms that air photo archaeology entirely missed (Figure 49). Given the increasing threat to village margins by housing

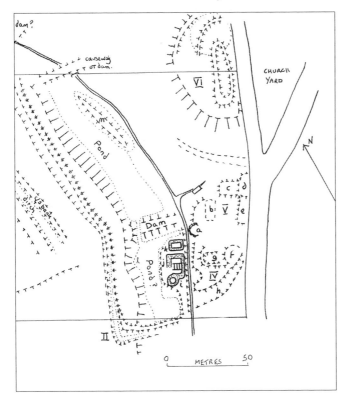

49 Church Brampton ponds and platforms. The features west of the churchyard at VI had previously been recorded, but the remains to the south, sparsely wooded and in the valley floor, escaped detection from air photos. At IV and V are groups of building platforms possibly indicating individual farmsteads. Structures at III, east of the lower pond, may represent a mill.

development and field enlargement, recording the fine detail of remains in and around villages is an ideal opportunity for local historians to engage with local history on the ground.

Figure 50 shows some fish pond dams (stippled), which lie on the valley floor immediately north of Moulton Church, near Northampton. They escaped detection for many years because they were obscured by hedgerows and scrub woodland, despite being described by the Northamptonshire historian Bridges in 1720. A, B and C are large ponds across the stream, while on a flood plain terrace to the north are three smaller ponds, D, E and F. D shares its dam with C, and there is a modern pond above it. Sticking to the ponds theme, Figure 51 shows a succession of ponds along a small stream (Harbourne River) near South Brent, Devon, where the detailed evidence has been added by annotation.

Figure 52 shows enclosure remains in one of those surviving open spaces north of the Griffin's Head pub in Mears Ashby, also near Northampton. The remains are complex with scarps at B1 to B4, and overlapping corners at A1 and A2; the site is another challenge for 'stratigraphy'. The writer's interpretation, shown below, suggests this was a rectangular enclosure in the north-west corner of the field, partly overlain by a building platform (broken line), which includes the corners A1 and A2.

I have included Bruce Motte in Lochmaben, also known as Lochmaben Old Motte, near Dumfries (Plate 29 & Figure 53) because this is a good illustration of

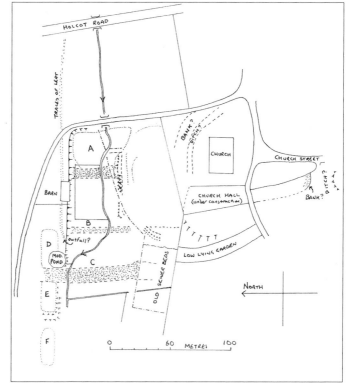

50 Moulton, near Northampton, Manor Ponds. Only the road causeway north of A was picked up as a possible dam on air photographs, in a Royal Commission Inventory in 1979, but under scrub and hedgerows the ponds described by Baker in 1720, A–F, were easily worked out.

looking around existing antiquities, as raised in the previous chapter. The view in Plate 29 is taken from Gallows Hill to the south, looking towards the motte, to the right, with figures on the summit, which lies within a golf course, on the southern edge of Lochmaben village. There is a further group of earthworks to the left of centre (C on Figure 53). However after taking that photograph I turned to look at the view south of Gallowhill, which to one side of the road is fields, and to the west golf course, as far as Castlehill Farm. Although the remains are low in profile, there are traces of a large oval enclosure, mostly reduced by ploughing, which appears to have been an annexe to Bruce Motte (Figure 53). The original motte belonged to the Bruce family, but was seized by Edward I who added a garrison camp and a deer park. It is usually thought that the garrison camp was under the later castle of Lochmaben at the south end of Castle Loch, but the Gallowshill site, on the ridge between Kirk Loch and Castle Loch, makes more sense.

Scottish border castles such as Dumfries (Figure 40), Lochmaben, Langholm (Figure 54), and Roxburgh (Figure 55 & Plates 30 & 31) were occupied for much of their useful life by English garrisons, which has somehow made them into archaeological untouchables. This is perplexing for local communities, particularly at Langholm, where locals cannot understand why their local history is allowed to rot in ignomiry. The writer has Border connections including a Lochmaben ancestor and particularly Langholm area ancestry (Hopes and Beatties in Westerkirk, who rode with the Armstrongs) which is a strong incentive to explore

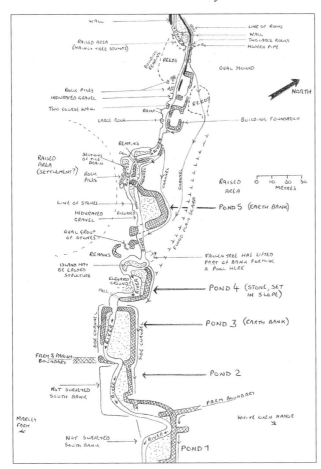

51 Annotated sketchplan of ponds along Harbourne River, near South Brent in Devon.

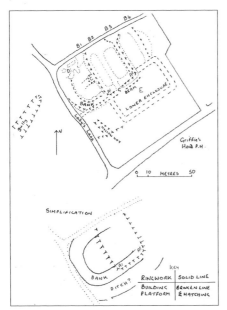

52 Mears Ashby, near Northampton. This complex of scarps and old walls in a small field in the heart of the village hides another problem of 'stratification', with overlying enclosures from different periods. In many villages such spaces have disappeared under modern housing.

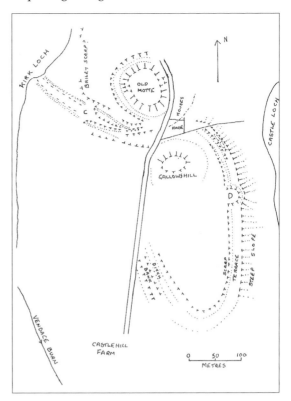

53 Bruce Motte, Lochmaben, Dumfriesshire with Gallows Hill annexe. This shows the original motte and the annexe noted by the writer extending south of Gallowshill.

Border castles (and an excuse to add all these illustrations to the end of the last chapter!).

At Langholm the site has been officially relegated to just the small ruined tower at A on Figure 54. However there are puzzling earthworks outside the fenced area at J, K and L on the south, and other remains under post-medieval house remains at F, G, H and I to the west, besides other features outside the encircling race track. Yet apparently Langholm Castle isn't open to discussion. I and others have explored the enigmatic remains around Roxburgh Castle with similar lack of official response. Plate 30 is more scenic than archaeological, but shows off the spectacular location, with the castle hill rising to the right of the River Teviot. Plate 31 is a view across the River Tweed, where there are lesser earthworks south-west at 1 and west at 2a and 2b on Figure 55. All these castles are part of local history to the people who live in the Scottish border counties, but mysteriously not archaeology.

The last sketch comes from the writer's original home territory of East Renfrewshire in Scotland, in this case definitely a village: the village of Eaglesham. Eaglesham was formerly a cluster of houses around a church at a cross-roads, but from 1771 to 1776 was remodelled to a plan by the 11th Earl of Eglinton and Winton. The plan was a figure A, with houses along the outside of the A and a crossroad above a cotton mill later erected in the lower part of this green. An exploration of the green space showed that the foundations of at least some of

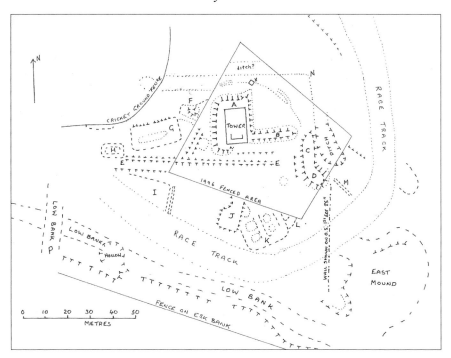

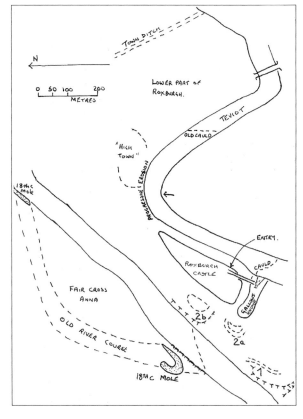

Above 54 Langholm Castle. The castle was seized by the English in 1544 and regained by the Scots in 1547 after a siege, as well as figuring in many other conflicts. That a mere tower (A), and a few enigmatic walls, are all that survives, makes no sense.

55 Roxburgh Castle, near Kelso. A ditched spur at 1 and other remains at 2a and 2b.

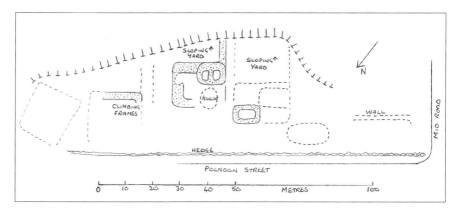

56 Eaglesham, near Glasgow, pre-1771 village. Foundations of the pre-1771 village found on the green of the planned village.

the pre-1771 cottages and yards still survived under grass within the green space (Figure 56).

Following watercourses

Having started with a stream in Chapter One at Tun Brook, it seems appropriate to end by mentioning the importance of exploring streams and valleys. Most villages will have a stream running through or close by, and even in limestone areas there may be a seasonal or former stream channel that has incised into the landscape in the past. It is also useful to identify significant springs. Water is an important resource in a village, for drinking, washing, brewing and sanitation. Where water is scarce, such as wells, springs or small rivulets there may be evidence of efforts to capture and conserve the limited resource. Where water is more plentiful, with a reliable stream or river nearby, there may be evidence of water power extraction. This may not be one site at the location of the most recent mill, but its medieval precursors, back to mills with horizontal water wheels, each with a different way of capturing and carrying water to the wheel, and choosing different locations for the mill. Some mills have sufficient water supply for several different functions at the same mill, such as snuff or fulling at a mill mainly devoted to grain. Elsewhere there may be different mill sites for each function. So that while there may be a mill or site or ruin of a former mill shown on Ordnance Survey maps, this is by no means the exclusive picture.

Watercourses may also be vital to local historians exploring intensively cultivated areas. It may look like all chance of surface remains surviving has been levelled by the plough, but water-courses, if they cannot be culverted, will survive as an oasis of trees and scrub in an otherwise sterile agricultural landscape. Together with the verges of old trackways, unspoiled ancient hedgerows, patches of woodland around old marl pits, ponds or abandoned farmsteads, these residual locations can offer clues to the landscape of the past. Earthworks entirely flattened in adjacent fields may still be visible in hedgerows or on the banks of streams. There may also be preserved old routeways, showing how people crossed the wider landscape, and even fragments of moats and other defensive works can be found on the banks of streams and on valley edges. We have come a long way from crossing Tun Brook in Chapter One, but at the end of the day watercourses often provide the answers.

NOTES

Chapter One

1. Hoskins, W.G. (1967) *Fieldwork in Local History*; Faber and Faber Ltd; Chapter One, 'Introduction to Fieldwork – A Backwoods Parish'
2. Welsh, T.C. (1989) *Eastwood District History and Heritage*; Eastwood District Libraries
3. Beresford, M. (1957) *History on the Ground*; Lutterworth Press
4. Beresford, M. (1954) *The Lost Villages of England*; Lutterworth Press
5. Aston, M. (1985) *Interpreting the Landscape – Landscape Archaeology and Local History*; Batsford; p18
6. Stephens, W.B. (1973) *Sources for English Local History: studies in the uses of historical evidence*; p29
7. Rogers, A. (1972; 2nd Edition 1977) *Approaches to Local History*; Longman; p1
8. *Ibid.*
9. Aston, M. and Rowley, R.T. (1974) *Landscape Archaeology: an introduction to fieldwork techniques on post-Roman landscapes*; David and Charles; p14
10. 'History on the Ground' in *Scottish Archaeological Gazette* 5 Spring 1984 p8–10
11. 'Nothing Ever Happened Here' *Scottish Archaeological Gazette* 11 Summer 1986 p10-13
12. Margary, I.D. (1957) *Roman Roads in Britain*; Phoenix House
13. Welsh, T.C. (1993) 'Evidence for the course of the Roman Road between Ribchester and Kirkham (Margary 703)' in *Archaeology North-West* no 5 Spring/Summer 1993 p10–13
14. Aston, M. (1985) *Interpreting the Landscape* p19
15. Currie, C.R.J. and Lewis, C.P. (1994) *English County Histories: A Guide*; Sutton
16. The Old and New Statistical Accounts of Scotland
17. E.g. Maitland Club and Bannatyne Club
18. New Statistical Account, Cathcart: the farmer found bones when attempting to plough the summit in 1840
19. Welsh, T.C. (1989) *Eastwood District History and Heritage* p56–58
20. Welsh, T.C. (1979) monograph East Kilbride and Carmunnock List of Antiquities p4
21. Welsh, T.C. (1971) *An Dunan, Kylesku Discovery and Excavation in Scotland* p47; NMRS NC23SW 1 contains the debate which followed. NMRS NC02NW 2 is the official account at Clachtoll.

Chapter Two

1. Aston and Rowley (1974) *op. cit.* p23
2. Aston (1985) *op cit.* p14
3. Aston and Rowley (1974) *op. cit*; Taylor, C. (1974) *Fieldwork in Medieval Archaeology*; Batsford
4. Aston and Rowley
5. Taylor, C. (1974) *op. cit.* Chapter Two; quotes from p23
6. Aston (1985) *op. cit.*; Brown, A. (1987) *Fieldwork for Archaeologists and Local Historians*; Batsford; Drewett, P.L. (1990) *Field Archaeology – An Introduction*; UCL Press; Chapter 3, notably pp42–50
7. Steane, J.M. and Dix, B.F. (1978) *Peopling Past Landscapes*; Council for British Archaeology; p61
8. Bowden, M. (1999) *Unravelling the Landscape: An Inquisitive Approach to Archaeology*; Tempus; p17–19
9. References to Newton (Nova Villa) in Dorset in Ballard, A. and Tait, J. (1923) British Borough Charters 1216–1307; Hoskins, W.G. (1955) *The Making of the English Landscape*; Hodder and Stoughton Ltd; p211–12 and 215–6, Beresford, M. and St Joseph, J.K.S. (1958) *Medieval England – An Aerial Survey* p225–6; Bowen, H.C. and Taylor, C. (1964) 'The site of Newton (Nova Villa), Studland, Dorset' in *Medieval Archaeology* Vol. VIII p223–26; PRO Calendar of Patent Rolls (1281–1292) p80, p217
10. Bowen and Taylor p224
11. *Ibid.* p225
12. Redeemed from the Heath, *Dorset Natural History and Antiquarian Society* Monograph 12 p91–93
13. Both Bowen and Taylor p226 and Hoskins p215–6 suggest reasons for failure
14. De Bosco in Gascony, Patent Rolls (1281–92) p231
15. Traskey, J.P. (1928) *Milton Abbey: a Dorset Monastery in the Middle Ages*; Calendar of Patent Rolls I p389/901

Chapter Three

1. Aston, M. (1985) *Interpreting the Landscape – Landscape Archaeology and Local History*; Batsford; p18
2. *Titchfield – A History* (1982) Polygraphic Ltd; *Titchfield – A Place in History* (1989) Ensign Publications, Titchfield History Society
3. Tate, W.E. (1946) *The Parish Chest*, 3rd Edition 1983 Phillimore; West, J. (1962) Village Records; 1997 Edition Phillimore
4. First Statistical Account Cathcart, Ross (1883) *Busby and its Neighbourhood*
5. Fraser, W. (1959) Memorials of the Montgomeries, Earls of Eglinton; nos 31–34, 63 and 77
6. The history is given in Welsh, T.C. (1989) *Eastwood District History and Heritage* p56–58
7. *Registrarum Monasteri de Passelet*. Maitland Club, Edinburgh 1832 (Reg de Pas) 101–2, 379–80
8. Strang, J.A. (1939) unpublished manuscript *A History of Mearns Parish* part 3, p417–20 translation
9. Scott, A.B. (1939) *Old Days and Ways in Newton Mearns*; Pickering and Inglis; p18 and 103–4; Welsh, T.C. (1992) 'The Renfrewshire Templelands' in *Renfrew Local History Forum Journal* Vol. 3

10. Bowen, H.C. and Taylor, C. (1964) 'The Site of Newton (Nova Villa), Studland, Dorset' *Medieval Archaeology* Vol. VIII p223–26; quotes p224 and 226; PRO Calendar of Patent Rolls (1281-1292) p217; Charter Rolls II p337

11. PRO Calendar of Inquisitions Post Mortem II 123, 404; Close Rolls 1227 p412; Calendar of Patent Rolls (1272 to 1281) p328; Coram Rege Roll 50, 56, 57, 60; Welsh, T.C. 'New Light on a missing 13th century new town in Dorset' *Medieval Settlement Research Group Annual Report* 7 p12–13; Welsh, T.C. (1998) 'Gotowre Super Mare: a New Town in Dorset commissioned 1286' *Somerset and Dorset Notes and Queries* Vol. XXXIV, Part 348 September 1998 p218–221

12. John Ainslie Eglinton Farm Plan 50 (Register House Edinburgh RHP 3/90-155); Crawford, W. (1834) Plan of the Barony of Eaglesham (RHP 10673/1); Welsh T.C. *Discovery and Excavation in Scotland* 1979, p36

13. Margary, I.D. (1957) *Roman Roads in Britain 4a*; Royal Military College Sandhurst's Museum holds a collection of these plans

14. Gentleman's Magazine 1836, part 1 p535; 1838 part 1 p192 and United Services Journal I

15. Codrington, T. (1903) *Roman Roads in Britain* 3rd Edition 1981 p238–239

16. Margary p86

17. Handasyd, T.B. (1783) Account of Antiquities found in the neighbourhood of Bagshot; *Archaeologia* Vol. 7, p199–202

18. National Monuments Record for Scotland NO12NW 9.08

19. *Reg Mag Sig* – Register of the Great Seal Vols V-VII

20. *Discovery and Excavation in Scotland* New Series Vol. 8 2007 p167; NMRS report acqu no 2007/138 and 198

21. Lee, H. (1715) manuscript history of Northampton transcribed by Baker, in Bodleian Library MS Top Northants; reproduced in *Journal of Northamptonshire Natural History Society and Field Club* Vol. 36, 67–76; 92–103, 145–152

22. Cox, F. (1899) The Borough Records of Northampton Vol. II p176

23. Northamptonshire Records Office NBC Deed Packet 611

Chapter Four

1. Bowden, M. (1999) *Unravelling the Landscape*; Tempus; p80

2. Taylor, C. (1974) *Fieldwork in Medieval Archaeology*; Batsford; p78

3. *Ibid.*

4. *Ibid.* p72/3

5. Welsh, T.C. (1999) Report: survey of selected sites in Glen Achall, Rhidorroch Wester Ross based on 1992 survey

6. Jobey, G. in *Discovery and Excavation in Scotland* 1966 p22; Trans. Dumfries and Galloway Nat. Hist and Ant. Soc ser 3 50 72–81

7. John Ainslie Eglinton Farm Plan 52; Welsh, T.C. (1973) *Discovery and Excavation in Scotland* p46

8. Baker, J. (1822–34) *History of Northamptonshire* Vol. I p343; *Inventory of the Historical Monuments of the County of Northampton*, Vol. III Fig 54; Edgar (1923) 'Borough Hill (Daventry) and its History' plan

9. Taylor, C. (1974) survey chapter; Bowden, M. (1999) Chapter Five

Chapter Five

1. Emmison, F.G. (1966) Archives and Local History; Methuen; p63
2. Harley, J.B. (1972) *Maps for the Local Historian − A Guide to the British Sources*; Blackfriars Press Ltd, Leicester
3. Hindle, P. (1988) *Maps for Historians*; Phillimore
4. Hindle (1998) p15−16
5. E.g. Gelling, M. (1978) *Signposts to the Past*; Phillimore and Co Ltd., Field, J. (1972) *English Field Names − A Dictionary*; David and Charles; also Grinsell, L.V. (1976) *Folklore of Prehistoric Sites in Britain*; David and Charles, which looks at place names
6. Brown, A. (1987) *Fieldwork for Archaeologists and Local Historians*; Batsford; Chapter 5
7. Taylor, C. (1974) Chapters 5 and 6

Chapter Six

1. Taylor, C. (1974) p17 and Brown, A. (1987) p14
2. Bowden, M. (1999) p37
3. Steane and Dix (1978) *Peopling Past Landscapes* p7−14
4. Aston, M. (1985) p19
5. Cheatle, J.R.W. (1976) *A Guide to the British Landscape*; Collins; p47
6. Toghill, P. (2000) *The Geology of Britain − an Introduction*; Airlife Books
7. Ashman, M.R. and Puri G. (2002) *Essential Soil Science− a Clear and Concise Introduction to Soil Sciene*; Blackwell
8. Huggett, R.J. (2007) *Fundamentals of Geomorphology*; Routledge Fundamentals of Physical Geography Series
9. Rackham, O. (1994) *History of the Countryside*; Weidenfeld and Nicolson; Rackham, O. (1976) *Trees and Woodland in the British Landscape*
10. Williamson, T. *Shaping Medieval Landscapes: Settlement, Society, Environment*; Wingatherer Press
11. Dark, P. (2000) *The Environment of Britain in the First Millennium* A.D.; Duckworth
12. Ingrouille, M. (1995) *Historical Ecology of the British Flora*; Chapman and Hall; Chapters 2 and 3
13. Darby, H.C. (1977) *Domesday England*; Cambridge University Press
14. Land Use Survey of Great Britain, Dudley Stamp
15. Bowden, M. (1999) p37
16. Welsh, T.C. (1999) unpublished report − Survey of Selected Sites in Glen Achall, Rhidorroch, Ullapool, Wester Ross
17. E.g. Tipping, R. and Halliday S. (1994) The age of alluvial fan deposition at Hopecarton in the upper Tweed valley, Scotland in *Earth Surface Processes and Landforms* 19, p333−348
18. Ballantyne, C.K. and Harris, C. (1994) *The Periglaciation of Great Britain*; Cambridge University Press
19. Evans, J.L. *An Introduction to Environment Archaeology*; Paul Elek Ltd
20. Brown, A. (1987) p69−70
21. Taylor p86
22. Ballantyne and Harris p74−5 including map on pingos
23. *Ibid.*

Chapter Seven

1. Taylor, C. (1979) *Roads and Tracks of Britian*; Dent & Sons Ltd; pxii
2. Watkins, A. (1974) *The Old Straight Track*; Abacus
3. Aston, M. (1985) p138
4. Margary, I.D. (1957) 2nd Edition p25
5. *Ibid.* p514
6. *Ibid.* on Lye Hill *etc.*
7. Unpublished report 29 October 1985 (fieldwork by permission Southwick Estates)
8. Margary, Edition 2 p74 and *Time Team* dig at Rowhook
9. Welsh, T.C.(1993) in Archeology NorthWest (5) 10-13
10. Margary, I.D. (1957) 2nd Edition p361-2 710b
11. Welsh, T.C. (1984) Road remains at Burbage and Houndkirk Moors, Sheffield – a possible Roman Road; *The Yorkshire Archaeological Journal*, Vol. 56 p27–31; the student who showed me the photograph is now Professor Paul Curran, Vice Chancellor of Bournemouth University
12. Jeffreys, T. (1771) *The County of York* 3rd Edition
13. Leader, J.D. (1877) *Roman Rotherham*
14. Guest (1879) *History of Rotherham*
15. Codrington, T. (1903) *Roman Roads in Britain*; Sheldon Press 3rd Edition p230
16. Margary, I.D. (1957) 2nd reprint p361-2; Margary based his route on a paper by F. Preston, who subsequently reverted to the route via Stanage Pole currently shown on maps
17. Barnatt, J. and Smith, K. (1997) *The Peak District – Landscape Through Time*; Windgatherer
18. A.E. and E.M. Dodd (1980) 2nd Edition revised and enlarged, *Peakland Roads and Trackways*; Moorland Publishing Co Ltd; p38
19. Dissertation by Carl Clayton 'The Roman road between Templeborough and Brough-on-Noe (Navio): an investigation into the theories and evidence of the possible routes.'
20. Welsh, T.C. *Ibid.*
21. Bishop Bennett cited in Lyson's *Magna Britannia* Vol I p201 *etc.*
22. *United Services Journal* (1836), p39
23. *Gentleman's Magazine* (1836) (1) 192–5
24. McDougall (1857) in Surrey Archaeological Collections Vol I p61-8
25. Codrington and to Margary 4a
26. Codrington p239
27. Margary p86
28. Norden, J. (1607) Map of Windsor Forest; version in Royal Library Windsor

Chapter Eight

1. Hoskins, W.G. *The Making of the English Landscape* p216–224 on Lammas lands
2. Dyos, H. J. (1961) *Victorian Suburb – a study of the growth of Camberwell*; Leicester University Press
3. Welsh, T.C. (1972) in *Discovery and Excavation in Scotland 1972*, p74; Royal Commission Inventory for the Lower Wards of Lanarkshire No 278
4. Welsh, T.C. (1989) *Eastwood District History and Heritage* p123; the mill is mentioned back to 1489, in 1575 John Coichtrane was miller; it was later known as Covenanter's Lint Mill

5. McDonald, H. (1854) *Rambles round Glasgow*; Hedderwick; p107
6. McDowall's History of the Burgh of Dumfries, section DUM p8; RCAHMS Inventory of Dumfriesshire p49–51; Barbour, J. (1905-6) The Castle of Dumfries; *Trans Dumfries and Galloway Natural History and Antiquarian Society* Vol. XVIII part 1 p48–93
7. Bain's Calendar of Documents Relating to Scotland Vol. II (1924)
8. According to a plaque at Abington Park Museum
9. Victoria County History
10. 1671 estate plan and a plan from 1820s
11. RCHM Inventory of Northamptonshire Vol. V (1985)
12. On display in Abington Park Museum, Northampton
13. Commons legislation in Chapter Seven of L.D. Stamp and W.G. Hoskins (1967) *The Common Lands of England and Wales*; Collins
14. Coles, J. (1837) *History and antiquities of Wellingborough*, p18

Chapter Nine

1. Finberg, J. (1958) *Exploring Villages*; Routledge and Kegan Paul Ltd; 3rd Edition 1998 Sutton
2. Hoskins, W.G. (1965) *The Midland Peasant – the Economic and Social History of a Leicestershire village*; MacMillan
3. Aston, M. and Rowley, T. (1974) *Landscape Archaeology – An Introduction to Fieldwork Techniques on Post-Roman Landscapes*; David and Charles; Chapter Six Fieldwork in Villages
4. Rowley, T. (1978) *Villages in the Landscape*; Dent
5. Aston, M.
6. Welsh, T.C. (1990) *Medieval Britain 1990*; Proposed Freckleton Bypass: Archaeological Evaluation of potential moated site, Lancaster University Archaeological Unit
7. Cunliffe-Shaw, R. (1949) *Kirkham in Amounderness*; Welsh, T.C. (1992) Possible prehistoric enclosures at Salwick and Treales, Fylde; *Archaeology North-West*, Autumn/Winter 1992 No4 p16–18

BIBLIOGRAPHY

Ashman, M.R. and Puri G. (2002) *Essential Soil Science – a Clear and Concise Introduction to Soil Science*; Blackwell

Aston, M. (1985) *Interpreting the Landscape – Landscape Archaeology and Local History*; Batsford

Aston, M. and Rowley, R.T. (1974) *Landscape Archaeology: an Introduction to Fieldwork Techniques on Post-Roman Landscapes*; David and Charles

Baker, J. (1822–34) *History of Northamptonshire*

Ballantyne, C.K. and Harris, C. (1994) *The Periglaciation of Great Britain*; Cambridge University Press

Ballard, A. and Tait, J. (1923) *British Borough Charters 1216–1307*

Barbour, J. (1905–6) The Castle of Dumfries; *Trans Dumfries and Galloway Natural History and Antiquarian Society* Vol. XVIII part 1 p48–93

Barnatt, J. and Smith, K. (1997) *The Peak District – Landscape through time*; Windgatherer

Beresford, M. (1954) *The Lost Villages of England*; Lutterworth Press

Beresford, M. (1957) *History on the Ground*; Lutterworth Press

Beresford, M. and St Joseph, J.K.S. (1958) *Medieval England – An Aerial Survey*

Bowden, M. (1999) *Unravelling the Landscape: An Inquisitive Approach to Archaeology*; Tempus

Bowen, H.C. and Taylor, C. (1964) 'The site of Newton (Nova Villa), Studland, Dorset' in *Medieval Archaeology* Vol. VIII p223–26

Brown, A. (1987) *Fieldwork for Archaeologists and Local Historians*; Batsford

Carrie and Hearne (1987) *Redeemed from the Heath*, Dorset Natural History and Antiquarian Society Monograph 12 p91–93

Cheatle, J.R.W. (1976) *A Guide to the British Landscape*; Collins Guides

Codrington, T. (1903) *Roman Roads in Britain* 3rd Edition 1981

Coles, J. (1837) *History and Antiquities of Wellingborough*

Cox, F. (1899) *The Borough Records of Northampton* Vol. II

Crawford, O.G.S. (1953) *Archaeology in the Field*; Phoenix House Ltd

Cunliffe-Shaw, R. (1949) *Kirkham in Amounderness*

Currie, C.R.J. and Lewis, C.P. (1994) *English County Histories: A Guide*; Sutton

Darby, H.C. (1977) *Domesday England*; Cambridge University Press

Dark, P. (2000) *The Environment of Britain in the First Millennium A.D.* Duckworth

Denman, D.R., Roberts, R.A. and Smith, H.J.F. (1967) *Commons and Village Greens – a study in land use, conservation and management*; Leonard Hill, London

Dodd, A.E. and E.M. (1980) 2nd Edition revised and enlarged, *Peakland Roads and Trackways*, Moorland Publishing Co. Ltd

Drewett, P.L. (1990) *Field Archaeology – An Introduction*; UCL Press

Dyos, H.J. (1961) *Victorian Suburb – A Study of the Growth of Camberwell*; Leicester University Press

Edgar (1923) *Borough Hill (Daventry) and its History*

Emmison, F.G. (1966) *Archives and Local History*; Methuen

Evans, J.L. *An Introduction to Environment Archaeology*; Paul Elek Ltd

Field, J. (1972) *English Field Names – A Dictionary*; David and Charles

Finberg, J. (1958) *Exploring Villages*; Routledge and Kegan Paul Ltd; 3rd Edition 1998 Sutton Publishing

Fraser, W. (1959) *Memorials of the Montgomeries, Earls of Eglinton*

Gelling, M. (1978) *Signposts to the Past*; Phillimore and Co Ltd

Grinsell, L.V. (1976) *Folklore of Prehistoric Sites in Britain*; David and Charles

Guest (1879) *History of Rotherham*

Handasyd, T.B. (1783) Account of Antiquities found in the neighbourhood of Bagshot; *Archaeologia* Vol. 7, p199–202

Harley, J.B. (1972) *Maps for the Local Historian – A Guide to the British Sources*; Blackfriars Press Ltd, Leicester

Hindle, P. (1988) *Maps for Historians*; Phillimore

Hook, D. (2000) *Landscape – the Richest Historical Record*; The Society for Landscape Studies

Hoskins, W.G. (1955) *The Making of the English Landscape*; Hodder and Stoughton Ltd

Hoskins, W.G. (1965) *The Midland Peasant – the Economic and Social History of a Leicestershire Village*; MacMillan

Hoskins, W.G. (1967) *Fieldwork in Local History*; Faber and Faber Ltd.

Huggett, R.J. (2007) *Fundamentals of Geomorphology*; Routledge Fundamentals of Physical Geography Series

Ingrouille, M. (1995) *Historical Ecology of the British Flora*; Chapman and Hall

Jeffreys, T. (1771) *The County of York* 3rd Edition

Leader, J.D. (1877) *Roman Rotherham*

Lee, H. (1715) manuscript history of Northampton transcribed by Baker, in Bodleian Library MS Top Northants; reproduced in *Journal of Northamptonshire Natural History Society and Field Club* Vol. 36, 67–76; 92–103, 145–152

McDonald, H. (1854) *Rambles round Glasgow*; Hedderwick

McDowall's *History of the Burgh of Dumfries*

Margary, I.D. (1957) *Roman Roads in Britain*

Newman, R. (2001) *The Historical Archaeology of Britain, c 1540–1900*; Sutton Publishing

Rackham, O. (1976) *Trees and Woodland in the British Landscape*; Phoenix

Rackham, O. (1994) *History of the Countryside*; Weidenfeld and Nicolson

RCAHMS Inventory of Dumfriesshire

Reed, M. (1990) *The Landscape of Britain from the beginnings to 1914*; Routledge

Rogers, A. (1972; 2nd Edition 1977) *Approaches to Local History*; Longman

Rowley, T. (1978) *Villages in the Landscape*; Dent

Scott, A.B. (1939) *Old Days and Ways in Newton Mearns*; Pickering and Inglis

Stamp, L.D. and W.G. Hoskins (1967) *The Common Lands of England and Wales*; Collins

Steane, J.M. and Dix, B.F. (1978) *Peopling Past Landscapes*; Council for British Archaeology

Stephens, W.B. (1973) *Sources for English Local History: Studies in the Uses of Historical Evidence*

Strang, J.A. (1939) unpublished manuscript *A History of Mearns Parish*

Tate, W.E. (1946) *The Parish Chest*, 3rd Edition 1983 Phillimore

Tavener, L.E. (1957) *The Common Lands of Hampshire*; Hampshire County Council

Taylor, C. (1974) *Fieldwork in Medieval Archaeology*; Batsford

Thirsk, J. ed (2000) *The English Rural Landscape*; Oxford University Press

Tipping, R. and Halliday, S. (1994) The age of alluvial fan deposition at Hopecarton in the upper Tweed valley, Scotland; *Earth Surface Processes and Landforms* 19, p333–348

Titchfield History Society (1982) *Titchfield – A history*; Polygraphic Ltd

Titchfield History Society (1989) *Titchfield – A Place in History*, Ensign Publications

Toghill, P. (2000) *The Geology of Britain – An Introduction*; Airlife Books

Traskey, J.P. (1928) *Milton Abbey: A Dorset Monastery in the Middle Ages*

Watkins, A. (1974) *The Old Straight Track*; Abacus

Welsh, T.C. (1984) Road remains at Burbage and Houndkirk Moors, Sheffield – a possible Roman Road; *The Yorkshire Archaeological Journal*, Vol. 56 p27–31

Welsh, T.C. (1989) *Eastwood District History and Heritage*; Eastwood District Libraries

Welsh, T.C. (1992) 'The Renfrewshire Templelands' in *Renfrew Local History Forum Journal* Vol. 3

Welsh, T.C. (1992) Possible prehistoric enclosures at Salwick and Treales, Fylde; *Archaeology North-West*, Autumn/Winter 1992 No4 p16–18.

Welsh, T.C. (1993) 'Evidence for the course of the Roman Road between Ribchester and Kirkham (Margary 703)' in *Archaeology North-West* no 5 Spring/Summer 1993 p10–13

Welsh, T.C. 'New Light on a missing 13th century new town in Dorset' *Medieval Settlement Research Group Annual Report* 7 p12–13

Welsh, T.C. (1998) 'Gotowre Super Mare: a New Town in Dorset commissioned 1286' *Somerset and Dorset Notes and Queries* Vol. XXXIV, Part 348 September 1998 p218–221.

West, J. (1962) *Village Records*; 1997 Edition Phillimore.

Williamson, T. (2004) *Shaping Medieval Landscapes: Settlement, Society, Environment*; Wingatherer Press

Wilson, D.R. (1982, 2nd Edition 2000) *Air Photo Interpretation for Archaeologists*; Tempus

INDEX

Other titles published by The History Press

Woods, Hedgerows and Leafy Lanes

RICHARD MUIR

The landscape of Britain has been shaped by hundreds of generations, yet in today's modern world it is rapidly being transplanted by concrete and tarmac. In this book renowned landscape detective Richard Muir shows how to spot the clues that can unravel the story of the countryside around us.

ISBN 9780752446158

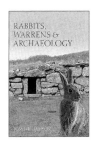

Rabbits, Warrens & Archaeology

TOM WILLIAMSON

Rabbit farming was a major industry in medieval and post-medieval Britian and the extensive archaeological traces it has left are often neglected or misinterpreted by archaeologists. This book provides a comprehensive summary of the remains and puts them firmly back on the archaeological map.

ISBN 9780752441030

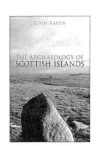

Scottish Odysseys: The Archaeology of Islands

EDITED BY GORDON NOBLE, TESSA POLLER, JOHN RAVEN AND LUCY VERRILL

Islands have long enthralled the minds of scholars. This book gathers together a selection of essays from an innovative conference, exploring the role of the island in art, literature, Bronze Age metalworking, Iron Age land administration, lairds' houses and the Mesolithic to Neolithic transition.

ISBN 9780752441689

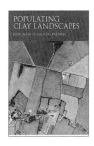

Populating Clay Landscapes

JESSICA MILLS AND ROG PALMER

Clay soils make up significant areas of Britian and Europe, though until recently little archaeological investigation has been undertaken on such soils. However they were often as densely populated as other areas. This book shows the importance of excavation and integration in adding to our knowledge of clay landscapes.

ISBN 9780752440965

Visit our website and discover thousands of other History Press books.

www.thehistorypress.co.uk